Animal Reiki Source presents

Animal Reiki Tails:
The Animal Reiki Source
Newsletter Collection
Volume II, 2006-2007

Edited by Kathleen Prasad

Disclaimer: Reiki is not intended as a substitution for professional veterinary care. Reiki sessions are given for the purpose of stress reduction and relaxation to promote healing. Reiki is not a substitute for medical diagnosis and treatment. Reiki practitioners do not diagnose conditions nor do they prescribe, perform medical treatment, nor interfere with the treatment of a licensed medical professional. It is recommended that animals be taken to a licensed veterinarian or licensed health care professional for any ailment they have.

Production: Linda Patrick
Cover Design: Maureen Mulhern

Published by: Animal Reiki Source
                  369-B Third St., #156
                  San Rafael, CA 94901
                  www.animalreikisource.com

ISBN: 978-0-578-04655-6

Table of Contents

Part 4: Reiki for Wild Creatures

Part 5: Teaching Animal Reiki

Part 6: Other Animal Reiki Topics

Introduction

Reiki and Animals: Creating a World of Wellness

By Kathleen Prasad
Originally published in *Reiki News Magazine,* Spring 2006

"Until one has loved an animal, a part of one's soul remains unawakened."

This quote, by celebrated French author Anatole France, captures in a nutshell the power and beauty of animals and the gifts they bring to our lives. In working with animals and Reiki, we open a window to this relationship; by connecting to animals energetically and being a part of their healing process, we are able to deepen our connection to the universe and our understanding of our place within it.

Reiki is ideal for use with animals because it is gentle and noninvasive. It works as a wonderful and safe complement to other systems of healing, both allopathic and holistic. It doesn't cause stress, discomfort, or pain, and yet yields powerful results. As highly sensitive and energetically aware beings, animals respond intuitively to Reiki's power in healing emotional, behavioral, and physical illnesses and injuries. In the deepest sense, Reiki helps the body heal itself. But even when a physical healing is not possible, Reiki can bring peace and comfort, and ease the transition to death. In addition, Reiki provides comfort and peace to surviving family members (both humans and animals) as they deal with the grief of loss. My student Michelle, for example, learned of Reiki just before her beloved cat, Ebony, passed away:

Traditional medicine had done all that it could. Inspired to help him in his last days, Michelle began to explore alternative healing options. Attracted by Reiki's ability to be given without direct contact, she began regular treatments for Ebony. After Reiki helped him pass with grace and peace, and without the pain that usually accompanied such [AN] illness, Michelle was faced with her own emptiness. Ebony had been her constant companion for more than 15 years, and she didn't know how to go on without him. With regular Reiki treatments for herself, Michelle was able to heal the grief and pain in her heart. She was so amazed at how much these treatments helped her in her time of deepest need, that she was inspired to learn to practice Reiki herself. Within a year, she had adopted a new kitten and begun giving her regular Reiki treatments as a regular part of their time together. With each treatment, her bond and understanding of her new kitty companion deepened. As Reiki brought healing and peace to both her new kitty and her own heart, it also brought a new understanding of the gifts animals could bring. And as her Reiki practice unfolded and expanded to become a central part of her life, and eventually her career, she came to realize that she would never have found this healing practice without Ebony. In bringing to her the most difficult lesson of life after loss, her treasured cat had truly guided her to her heart's calling.

Reiki works even in extremely stressful environments, like animal shelters, bringing a sense of calm to the animal recipient. The story of one shelter dog I treated comes to mind:
The shelter dog jumped, circled and barked incessantly, unable to relax in the stressful new environment of the kennel. He had recently been removed from his home due to abuse and neglect, and it appeared that he had never felt the gentle touch of a human hand. His ribs poked through his sides, and his body was covered in wounds, both old and new. I sat in the lotus position, just outside the kennel, put in my earplugs and closed my eyes, silently letting the dog know I was here to help him. Keeping my eyes averted in respect, I began to offer him Reiki energy through the wire mesh of his cage, letting him know he need take only the energy he was open to. Almost immediately, the dog stopped jumping and approached the bars carefully, staring at me briefly before retreating to the other side of the kennel. After just a few more jumps, barks, and circling by me to sniff curiously, he began to yawn and his eyelids became heavy. Within a few more minutes, he had stopped barking completely and come to the

side of the kennel nearest to me again. This time, after giving me a meaningful gaze and plopping down on his side, he leaned his body against the bars, let out a huge sigh, and settled into a relaxing Reiki nap.

This is just one of the many examples of how Reiki can build trust and bring stress-relief and relaxation to even the most stressful situations. In this way, Reiki practitioners often find themselves serving as harbingers of peace and harmony. In offering healing to the animals, we offer a rebalancing not only to animals themselves, but also to the human/animal bond. In learning the language of energy, with the help of the animals, we can learn to live closer to their world, to nature and to the earth. As the above story illustrates, when approached with respect and gentleness, regardless of what their previous experiences with humans may be, animals can learn to trust again in the peaceful harmony provided by a Reiki treatment. Humans, too, can learn to trust the subtle yet powerful possibilities of Reiki's healing energy.

According to Dr. Lauren Chattigre, DVM, DVetHom, CVA, CVCP, Reiki Master, of the Cascade Summit Animal Hospital in West Linn, Oregon, openness to Reiki hinges on people's acceptance of the unknown. "It's just a question of people getting used to the idea, of people trying it and seeing the benefits. Change is slow, especially in scientific circles, you know. Acupuncture used to be not nearly as accepted as it is now. It's just been a matter of time and trial and education and people trying it."

A growing number of veterinarians around the world are opening their minds and even offices to Reiki. For example, holistic veterinarians in the United Kingdom work in conjunction with Reiki practitioners, providing referrals and support. In the United States alone, nearly 100 veterinarians are listed as Reiki practitioners with the American Holistic Veterinary Medical Association (www.ahvma.org).

Dr. Chattigre practices veterinary medicine using both conventional and alternative methods. She uses Acupuncture, Chiropractic, Homeopathy, and Reiki to support the health and well-being of her animal clients. "Reiki, though, is a tougher sell. Because it's more out there. Acupuncture, you can see a needle going in; chiropractic, you can see something moving. But Reiki is a little tougher for people to accept."
Nonetheless, her clients, when open to Reiki, have seen wonderful results. Dr. Chattigre remembers one Reiki client, "a very young dog who had to have bilateral hip surgery and I did Reiki after each. They didn't do both surgeries at the same time; they did one and allowed it to heal, and did the other and allowed it to heal, and the Reiki sessions started out in person, I went to her house. But after a time, we did those by distance as well. And later on, when they re-X-rayed the area to just monitor the healing, apparently the surgeon was quite impressed with the speed of healing and he said, 'What are you doing for this dog?' and she tried to explain, and he said, 'Well, whatever you're doing, just keep doing it!' "

Dr. Chattigre also recalls a feline client who responded particularly well to Reiki. "He had recurrent urinary crystals, mostly because of stress. And a lot of kitties get crystals from stress, but he particularly was a very high-stress kitty. And the client could not bring him into the clinic, because he had that much trouble coming in specifically. So for him, I actually did distance Reiki, where I would sit in a room quietly in the vet clinic, and he would be at his house, and there are ways in Reiki practice where you send the energy of Reiki long-distance. And during the session, we would set up a time so that she [the cat's person] knew and I knew. The cat would just be doing his thing, but she often commented that at that time, he would become very quiet, not fall asleep per se, but just become quiet and thoughtful, and afterward he would be much calmer. So she would just call me periodically for a distant Reiki session when he seemed to be getting a little more uptight." With regular distant Reiki treatments, he was able to remain crystal-free.

For veterinarian Carolina Kliass of Sao Paulo, Brazil, it's all a matter of letting people see the results Reiki can produce. In her private practice, Dr. Kliass uses conventional veterinary techniques in addition to Reiki, and occasionally flower essences and Homeopathy.

Dr. Kliass fondly remembers, one story of "a client I'll never forget. She was a Boxer; she was 10 years old, and passed away two months ago. And she was very special because all the responses that you want from a person or a dog, or animal—that you'd expect from Reiki—she gave to me. All the responses." Each time Dr. Kliass visited the dog's home for a Reiki treatment, "she turned and went to the special place that always we did Reiki. We always did Reiki there, or on the ground near the sofa or on the sofa. And she lay down and looked at me and said, 'I'm here, work on me.' It was so fun; she was amazing. She always respected the Reiki sessions; it was very nice. She was my darling. She was wonderful."

Besides the warm emotional response the Boxer gave to Dr. Kliass during treatments, the dog responded well physically to treatments. "She had bone cancer, and the evolution was not so fast as was expected, because it's a very aggressive disease, and it took more than a year until she passed away," says Dr. Kliass. "And she was taking homeopathic remedies, too, but without Reiki, I think this period would be shorter, absolutely. A few months." Dr. Kliass believes the dog's quality of life during her year of Reiki treatments was also enhanced: "This year period, she was great. She lived on a farm: a ranch, all hills up and down, and she walked all around with this cancer in her leg."

Treatment Guidelines

When offering Reiki to your animal, there are two options for treatments: in-person Reiki (for Level 1 through Master Level practitioners) and distant Reiki (for Level 2 and Master Level practitioners).

Offering Reiki in person to your animal means being in the same room with him as you give a treatment. When choosing this kind of treatment, find a familiar and comfortable place where your animal is free to move within the room, without constraints. In addition, always ask his permission before you begin. By giving your animal freedom and choice in treatment, you build trust and acceptance. Many animals enjoy hands-on treatments, and will come forward and put their bodies under your hands. In these cases, use the hand positions that seem comfortable and pleasing to your animal. Often, hands-on treatments may involve only one or two hand positions. Remember that Reiki will go where it needs to go, and the most important role for you is to be an open channel for the energy. That's one of the lessons I learned after volunteering at BrightHaven, a non-profit, holistic animal retreat in Sebastopol, California:

> In working with the senior and special needs animals at BrightHaven, I learn something new from my animal teachers every visit! When I arrive, I find a seat in one of the rooms, center myself and ask whatever animals want and need healing to come; I mentally let them know that I am there to offer healing to whoever is open to it. In the beginning, I expected the most fragile cats to shy away from the stronger feeling of hands-on Reiki, and the stronger, healthier ones to approach me. But time and time again, the most fragile ones are the ones who climb into my lap the moment I arrive and stay there until I leave. Sometimes, they are too sick to even walk, and they will simply lift their head and stretch toward me, trying to come closer. The key is, I believe, that I have allowed them to approach me, to CHOOSE Reiki for themselves, thus honoring their unique and individual ways of receiving it.

> For some animals, treatments are much more comfortable from a few feet away, or even from across the room or paddock, and by allowing your animal to come and go from your hands according to his

preference, you will ensure an enthusiastic response! Allow 30 to 60 minutes for optimum results. The more you work with animals, the easier this will become.

The second option for treating your animal is through distant healing. Distant Healing is very effective and can be preferable to hands-on treatments in some instances.

It is wonderful to be able to send your animal Reiki when you are away from him. And some animals may be extremely small, fearful, old and fragile, or close to death and may be better able to relax and absorb Reiki when you are out of their presence. Allow 20 to 30 minutes for optimum results.

Distant Reiki offers the same benefits as hands-on Reiki: physical, emotional, and spiritual healing. Because we are all one at the most basic, energetic level, healing distantly is not so much "sending energy" as it is remembering and "truly knowing" this connection of all things.

Mattie is an older, beautiful lab mix. He received a series of four distant treatments for stiffness and difficulty walking in his hind end. The first treatment I sent to him began with my focusing on his photo and asking of his permission to send healing. The energy flowed very gradually at first, and I could tell he was still getting used to the feeling of the energy. I reassured him that he need take only the energy he was comfortable receiving: that this treatment was on HIS terms. By the end of the first treatment, I felt the energy flowing very strongly to him. Sure enough, his person said that he paced during the first half of the treatment, finally settling down and resting at the end. On the subsequent three treatments, however, once he had assessed the energy and trusted that he could take the energy in the ways he was comfortable, he settled more quickly each time, finally sleeping through the entire fourth treatment. His person happily relayed to me that he showed immediate improvement in the balance and coordination of his hind end in his daily walks.

In distant Reiki, energy is sent mentally, either using intention, or sometimes using a photo or surrogate to represent the client. A distant Reiki treatment can provide pain relief for various illnesses and injuries, accelerated healing from surgery, emotional healing, including healing for behavioral issues, prevention of illness or accelerated healing of an illness, and can greatly ease the transition to death. Distant Reiki is also helpful in healing family situations that may involve your animal and in helping human companions with the process of an animal's death. A distant treatment can also be sent to heal a traumatic event in your animal's past.

Looking Forward to the Future

As more people, including veterinarians, educate themselves about the options of complementary healing modalities such as Reiki, more and more animals will benefit. But on a deeper level, as humans experience the healing possibilities of energetic connection with animals, a new and deeper understanding of our relationship with each other and place in the universe will result. By offering animals the gift of Reiki peace and harmony, you open yourself to the possibility of living in a world of respect and reverence for all creatures: a world of true balance and wellness.

Finding the Optimum Treatment Program

Although sometimes healing can be seen in one or two treatments, for continued health, balance and well-being, all animals benefit most from a regularly scheduled program of Reiki. Remember, while Reiki is a powerful healing system on its own, it is also a wonderful complement to other therapies that may be helping your animal recover. It is not meant as a substitute for veterinary care. In addition to providing Reiki treatments for your animal, always consult your trusted veterinarian about the best course of medical treatment.

Equine, Canine and Feline Reiki Treatment Programs:

- For horses in full training (endurance, dressage, etc.), working, agility, or show dogs, and show cats: Begin with a series of four treatments on consecutive days, then once a week or every other week for maintenance. Daily treatments suggested on the most demanding of days.

- For horses in rehab and dogs and cats recovering from injury/illness: Begin with a series of at least four treatments on consecutive days, followed by once or twice a week until recovery.

- For horses in retirement, and senior dogs and cats: Begin with a series of four treatments on consecutive days, followed by once a week or every other week for maintenance.

- For horses, dogs, and cats nearing their transition: Begin with a series of treatments on consecutive days, followed by a few times a week or as needed for support in this process.

Small Animal/Avian Reiki Treatment Programs:

- Health maintenance: Begin with a series of four treatments on consecutive days, followed by once a week or every other week for maintenance.

- Recovery from illness/injury: Daily treatment or as often as needed until recovery.

- Seniors: Begin with a series of four treatments on consecutive days, followed by once a week or as needed for maintenance.

- Nearing their transition: Daily treatments or as needed for support with this process.

Part 1:
Reiki for Small Animals

Aimee the Rabbit:
A Story of Healing

By Sue Mallory

As a Registered Nurse in a small Nursing Home I have always looked for different ways to help my patients. There are always a wide variety of conditions to manage. And no matter how hard you try there are always limitations to medications and life in an institution. I learned about Reiki through a fellow nurse. Three of us got together to learn Level 1. We then spent the next few months looking at ways to incorporate this modality into our practice. During this time and while obtaining my Level 2, I began to wonder why I couldn't apply this knowledge and skill to family pets. Everyone I asked thought it was a great idea but nobody I asked here in Toronto seemed to be venturing into that direction.

I began to experiment at a Parrot Rescue. I knew I would be eaten alive if I tried to put my hands on the testy Macaws. For the reason of simple self-preservation I began to use Reiki energy at a distance and noticed different results. It was clear to me that the birds were aware and able to feel the energy.

While at work one day, my dear friend Shanlee sat down beside me at the Nurse's Station and began to tell me about her pet rabbit Aimee. Shanlee was terribly worried as Aimee had a bowel obstruction, a very grave condition in rabbits. It appeared that thoughts of euthanasia were beginning to surface in the minds of Shanlee and the local vet. I too have been terribly worried about a beloved pet, so was anxious to offer assistance. I offered to give Aimee a Reiki treatment after work. Friday evening Shanlee and I left work and went to her apartment so I could try Reiki on the much-loved bunny.

When we arrived at Shanlee's apartment Aimee was tucked inside a small wooden box on the floor. Apparently, it's one of those things rabbits like to tuck themselves into - Aimee just fit. Facing the bunny on the floor, her body stretched out in front of me, I began to offer Reiki. I was immediately struck by what I would call "distortion" of the energy. Aimee was clearly drawing more on her right side than her left. When I finished the treatment and voiced my findings to Shanlee I was informed that the right side was the location of the obstruction.

The next day at work Shanlee informed me that Aimee began to exhibit some odd behavior after I had left for home. Apparently, while in her box, she kept turning 180 degrees about every 5 minutes. The turns were always in the same direction and lasted for about 30 minutes. The bunny then settled in for the night.

I performed Reiki again Saturday and Sunday evening. Once, while Shanlee was holding Aimee and I was giving a treatment, the bunny became so relaxed her head lolled to the side and she was almost motionless for a few minutes. By the end of the treatment Sunday night I was struck by the difference in the way Aimee was drawing energy. What was once distorted was now clearly even on both sides.

I was greatly intrigued by this observation. Born in North America and being a Registered Nurse for over a decade I have been firmly entrenched in the beliefs of Western medicine. There is always a tiny piece of me that pooh-pooh's this "other stuff". You know what people would call "a bunch of nonsense," and "mumbo jumbo". Aimee was taking medication prescribed by the vet and that is naturally where my mind went - perhaps the medications were finally "kicking in". However, as I drove home that Sun night there were thoughts that kept bouncing around in my head. There had been no previous sign of the medications "kicking in". Plus, I couldn't let go of the difference in the flow of energy in three days. Had I stumbled onto something? Or did I just want it so bad?

By Monday morning Shanlee informed me that the vet had phoned and wanted to see Aimee that evening. I was becoming increasingly worried that this would be the end. It would never occur to me to interfere, but I felt very strongly we had to wait until Wednesday to make a decision. On our way to the appointment I suggested that if the vet wanted euthanasia that we ask about the ramifications of waiting a few more days. Aimee got a thorough examination, and our spirits lifted when the vet announced that things were no longer grave - in short - things were moving in the right direction. We took the bunny home and kept right on doing the same things. Shanlee kept up with the basic needs and I kept doing Reiki.

Well, if you remember, I had felt very strongly that we had to wait until Wednesday. While up in the wee hours of Thursday morning I noticed there was a message on my phone. I had apparently missed it the night before. The message was from Shanlee: just two words, "She pooped." I mean really, what more needed to be said?

It took probably another two weeks for Aimee to completely recover. I had stopped doing Reiki as I no longer felt it was needed - the crisis had clearly passed. A few weeks later during a chat, Shanlee remarked that Aimee had totally healed. In addition to her physical recovery there was a huge change in her behavior. Aimee had come to live with Shanlee after spending at least three months in a cage at the local Animal Shelter. She was never crazy about people getting too close, and definitely not happy about being picked up. Now, after her Reiki experiences, she allows her mom Shanlee to hold her much longer and has been known to bounce into a nearby lap for possible apple opportunities. Best of all, she allows her mom to attach a pink Barbie collar and pink leash for the daily walk down to Lake Ontario.

About a month after this health episode, I was visiting Shanlee and my favorite bunny. Just before I was about to leave, Aimee was at my feet. As I bent down to rub and kiss her nose I wondered at her close proximity and thought maybe she had just come to say thank you.

About the Author: Sue Mallory is a Registered Nurse and Reiki Level 2 Practitioner in Toronto, Canada. You can contact her at nursesoo@rogers.com.

Reiki Reflections On 2005

Marbles

By Chrissie Slade

Reiki Training

Looking back at 2005 made me realize what an exciting and busy year it was! In April I became a Usui Reiki Master and in June I became a Karuna Reiki Master. Both courses were magical and during the training we all learned so much from working with the Reiki energy, from the wisdom of the Reiki Masters, and also from sharing information and experiences with each other. I also worked with Kathleen via email and on the phone during the year. The knowledge and enthusiasm that she shared with me has proved to be invaluable for both treating and training. It just goes to show that distance is no barrier to increasing your knowledge!

My First Reiki 1 Course

At the end of November 2005 I took the plunge and taught my first Reiki 1 course. There were three students, all of whom I had met via their guinea pigs! At the beginning of the day, all three were apprehensive that they wouldn't be able to "do Reiki". By the end of the day everyone went home knowing that the energy was there for him or her to use whenever they wanted. We shared an exciting day learning about Reiki, doing a Chakra Meditation and doing practical sessions on each other and of course the guinea pigs. Three "willing little volunteers" were offered Reiki. They soon started getting used to the energy and showed signs of total relaxation. Feedback from the course was excellent, and I am looking forward to offering more courses this year.

Major Operations

The last few months of 2005 were very stressful as two of my guineas needed major surgery. We are lucky enough to have a fantastic guinea pig vet who is also a brilliant surgeon, but nevertheless, time seems to stop when you are waiting for the phone call to say that everything is OK.

In August, Marbles had a bladder stone removed. He went to the vets with his friend Florence to keep him company, as well as being sent Reiki by 5 Reiki Masters! A little over the top maybe, but Marbles sailed through the operation and 5 minutes after coming round from the operation he was happily eating cucumber! The vet had never seen a pig recover so quickly from the anesthetic, and when I went to collect Marbles, apart from a shaved tummy and a small incision, you would not know that he'd had a major operation. His recovery was swift with the help of daily Reiki, but unfortunately he grew another bladder stone just 6 weeks after the original operation. He had a second operation, which was a total success, but this time his recovery was much slower due to the fact that his little body was only just getting over the first operation and anesthetic. When he came home he was in a bad way and I spent most of the evening giving him Reiki. After a couple of days he turned the corner and soon started to put on the weight he had lost. At the time of writing Marbles is fit, well and has made it to 20 weeks with no reoccurrence of stones.

In November, Gucci the gorgeous golden guinea had a major problem with is right eye. Literally overnight it had swelled up and

the conjunctiva was completely outside the eye. He was whisked to the emergency vet and received anti-inflammatory pain relief, antibiotics and eye drops. The next day the eye looked even worse, so we went to see our normal vet and unfortunately the eye needed to be removed. Gucci sailed through the operation with a little help from 4 Reiki Masters and made a swift recovery. The cause of the problem turned out to be an abscess behind the eye, so no amount of antibiotics or eye drops would have helped. Within a week he was all healed up and getting on with his life. Animals just don't seem to have the same hang-ups about "disability" as us humans.

Never Give Up Hope

At the beginning of December, Mr. Nosey was diagnosed as having a tumor. He is just 3 and I had only adopted him a year before, so it was a bit of a shock. Guinea pigs with tumors generally don't last very long, but just because veterinary medicine only had pain relief on offer didn't mean that I was about to give up on this precious pig! After a good few hours of research on the Internet, I formulated a plan to try and help his little body to start healing itself. Mr. Nosey gets 30 minutes of Reiki a day as well as some extra vitamins, herbs and Colloidal Silver. I also set up a Reiki Crystal Grid for him, and give him water with various crystals (charged with Reiki) in it. He has also been attuned him to Reiki as it seemed to be the right thing to do to help him to heal himself. I picked 1st January 2006 for the attunement, as it was the beginning of a new year and also a Full Moon. Mr. Nosey's lowest point was in the middle of December when he was sleeping a lot, down to 2 lbs 4 oz (from 2 lbs 12 oz) and looking hunched up and miserable. Day by day he started to improve. At the time of writing he weighs 2 lbs 8 oz, has much more energy and is a happy boy again. Whilst I wouldn't like to claim that he is "cured", there is certainly a healing process going on, and Reiki has played a big part in this.

My life would definitely be incomplete without Reiki and the unconditional love of my guinea pigs. It is wonderful to know about the healing power of Reiki and to have regular reminders that it really does work.

2009 Update:

Marbles continued to be well for the next 3 years. There were no more bladder stones and no further vet visits until his last week; he died peacefully in my arms

Mr. Nosey & Mr. Cool

a couple of months after his 6th birthday. Marbles was loved by everyone who met him and was a regular participant in all my Reiki courses. He was a little Reiki sponge and loved the attention that he received from all the students. He left a big hole in my heart when he departed, but his spirit lives on and will soon be honored with a new website:)

Gucci lived happily for another 3 years after his operation and was never bothered by his "disability." He was a very loving guinea and in his time with me he had three lovely wives - Scruffy, Allegra and Pashca. When Scruffy and Allegra went on to their next lives, he moved on very quickly with the help of Reiki. In both cases he saw the body - guinea pigs do have some level of understanding about death and dying. So for those of you with guineas, always show them the body of any friends that they have lived with who may have passed. Each time he was allowed to choose his next wife and made excellent choices both times:)

Mr. Nosey continued to do well for the whole of 2006. He had a lovely summer, spending a lot of time out on the grass having fun with his brother Mr. Cool. At the beginning of 2007 he started to go downhill again and had to be helped on his way on Easter Saturday 2007. Mr. Nosey had survived for 16 months after he was diagnosed with a tumor, and required no further vet visits until his last day. Neither of my vets could believe that he had survived for so long, and neither vet could offer explanation as to how he did! Guineas with tumors usually go downhill very quickly and rarely last more than a few weeks after diagnosis, so I feel sure that the supportive therapies that he received really helped him.

About the Author: Chrissie Slade lives in Reading, England with her 10 Gorgeous Guineas and partner Sam. She came into contact with Kathleen after discovering her wonderful website. In the UK there is not nearly as much information about Animal Reiki as Chrissie would like, so she has just started putting together her new website: www.animal-reiki.com The focus of her work will continue to be with animals, but she always acknowledges that humans enjoy Reiki too. She can be reached at www.gorgeousguineas.com.

Part 2:
Reiki for Dogs

The Remarkable Recovery of "Ribs"

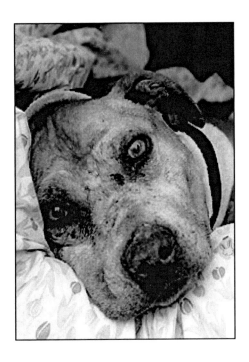

By Patricia Monahan Jordan, DVM, CVA, CTCVH and Herbology

While at the RAVS (Rural Area Veterinary Services) this year, I was able to do two Reiki treatments on a very special dog. This trip was to White River, Arizona on the Apache Reservation. There were veterinary students present from all over the country and world: Ireland, England, Scotland, Canada and Sri Lanka, and from the United States--New Mexico, Arizona, California and me from North Carolina. They really need volunteers from all walks of veterinary practice and it is an experience that you will never forget. As volunteers, we help deal with the pet overpopulation problem and those who are even more economically challenged than our own

areas. The trip becomes a crash course in MASH units and disaster medicine. I saw things that I only was aware of from textbooks!

In proper recognition, this dog had been undergoing conventional treatment by very involved veterinary students, technicians and his primary RAVS veterinarian. However, his spirit was so broken when I saw him, I nicknamed him Ribs. I talked at length with his RAVS veterinarian, who was discussing having him put down. I found additional pathological problems on the dog that needed to be worked on by a chiropractor. Since the talk was more toward putting him down, I spent time directly with the patient, and found the "giving up attitude" had transferred to the patient.

My Reiki treatment focused on the patient, the emotional abuse he had faced, the desire of the present caretakers to have the patient survive, the "giving up" attitude of the veterinarian handling the case, the presence of the spinal subluxations, the GI issues and the fact that whomever had done these things to him would be karmically taken care of. I prayed that the caretakers that wanted to care for him would step up to the plate with handling the responsibilities of his care. In addition, I explained to the patient that I understood these people both wanted him and wanted to help take care of him.

There was little response from the patient the first treatment however, with the second he came to me for it and bumped into me for hands-on Reiki. He was so appreciative! A dramatic energetic shift occurred so that amazingly enough, the next day his GI issues stopped, and he started prancing around. Wonderfully, his people called the vet asking for him back and said that they were ready to do whatever it took to help him heal. As soon as the patient knew that he was wanted and that he was going home, his whole attitude and physical self changed even more for the better. The conventional vet was confused by the sudden positive resolution, but took the patient back to his people. And so, very good and thank you Reiki: Ribs made it back to his family instead of being put to sleep.

About the Author: Please see end of next story for details about Dr. Jordan.

The Wonderful Recovery of Po

By Patricia Monahan Jordan, DVM, CVA, CTCVM & Herbology

Recently sent from a puppy mill to a local pet store, Po the pup was diagnosed with his problem after an upper respiratory infection got so bad he blew out a lung coughing. Radiographs showed that not only was one lung collapsed, but also that his heart was very abnormal. He also had a really bad cough, would not eat and was in such bad shape that he was set to be euthanized. It didn't help any that he was so tiny. Pet stores seem to want tinier and tinier pups because the public seems to want them. Shame, because the cross-country trip to the store, their fragile status in general, and the over medicating and vaccinating leave them almost defenseless. The pup was less than 2 pounds and really, really on his way to checking out. The main reason they handed him to me to treat was they couldn't get him to eat.

My first meeting with him was to just ask him if he wanted help and he came directly to me and got under my hands! I cupped him right on top left under his chest and did Reiki for a few minutes. He would have taken more but I had a lot to do once summoned. I quickly finished with the Power symbol and a whisper that I would continue distantly from another part of the hospital while I was working with other patients.

I did another treatment hands-on later in the day at the beginning of lunch. The pup so tiny and weak, but really perked up when he saw me, coming right over to me. I set his chest elevated when I left as it helped his ability to breath.

When I got complete control of his case the next day I stopped all of his medications. They had put him on very strong antibiotics and cough suppressants and many unneeded medications.

I gave him only NutriCal by syringe which he relished and consumed well. Reiki hands-on and off was given. Every day for the next five days I treated him at the hospital. I took him home with me for the weekend and did much-needed TLC at home, also hygiene, clips, baths, and better food.

At first I got him on Royal Canine kibble for minis and now he is eating some Wellness, some Spots Stew by Halo and also I have made him homemade raw food which is his favorite: free ranged white turkey hamburger (no antibiotics, hormones or drugs!) mixed with a premium quality organic baby food of spring vegetables (processed) mixed with Braggs amino acid flavoring and Happy Heart supplements of chicken breast jerky fortified with flax and taurine.

Not only did his lung heal, but also his heart issue mostly resolved; although he is not yet cured completely, I have no doubt that he will get there.

The next weekend he was sleeping with me when he got very strong hiccups. I used Reiki to stop the hiccups and later noticed that the cough that he had was gone after that night! This was amazing to me, so the second set of radiographs were taken to see where he was.

I took additional rads two weeks later--amazing results!

He now weighs 2.7 lbs, eats like a horse not a Maltese pup. I took him walking on Sunday last and he did a quarter of a mile without any problems--I picked him up and carried him for the rest of my walk, mainly because I thought his little legs had done enough for the day.

He drags around my heavy work boots for fun and that is hilarious because the boots are five times his size. Right now he is sacked out on the couch. You can't really keep him confined anymore--he must have been a mountain climber in another life. I named him "Po" which is the Chinese word for soul. He didn't look like he would make it but wow, look at him now.

About the Author: Patricia Monahan Jordan is a 1986 graduate of the North Carolina College of Veterinary Medicine. Having practiced conventional veterinary medicine for fifteen years and originated three different veterinary practices in North Carolina, Dr. Jordan found Holistic medicine in 2000 at the AHVMA American Holistic Veterinary Medical Association Conference in Williamsburg, VA. Until the AHVMA meeting, many, many dead ends were predictably showing up in cases treated conventionally. Holistic medicine ignited a pathway towards many of the modalities that provided this veterinarian with the inspiration to follow the path of healing with energy and intention. Completing a Master's Program in TCVM Traditional Chinese Veterinary Medicine with Dr. Xie of the Chi Institute and participating in Dr. Richard Pitcairn's Professional Course for Veterinarians has opened the way to naturopathic medicine for Dr. Jordan. Memberships in the AHVMA, the VBMA Veterinary Botanical Medicine Association, AVH Academy of Veterinary Homeopathy have also provided her with a much wider range of healing options. Reiki I and II were taught to Dr. Jordan by Kathleen Prasad and in Dr. Jordan's words, "it was this energy work that has allowed me to move past just the physical and channel healing for the nonphysical, the emotional, mental and spiritual, a communication that addresses the entire macrocosm and for the purpose of the highest good. We never learned that in conventional training!" You can contact Dr. Jordan at: patriciamonahanjordan@hotmail.com

Reiki Worms My Heart

Lisa offers Reiki to an equine client

By Lisa Chapman-Sorci

Late one evening I received an emergency call from a woman named Bonnie who needed help for her beloved German Shepard, James. Several months earlier, James had been diagnosed with heartworms. The vet took the standard measures, but unfortunately, the condition progressed into Advanced Heartworm Disease. This beautiful, once healthy and athletic dog had become very sick and weak and spent much of his time in what must have been excruciating pain. The vet gave James a grim prognosis.

James' humans requested that I use Reiki energy so that it might alleviate the pain and give James comfort until they could get him to their conventional vet the next day.

When I arrived at their home, James was in pain with labored breathing. He was lying in the middle of the room in a huge pile of pillows. I introduced myself and he allowed me to not only place my hands on him (and his belly that was swollen from medication), but after a while, I snuggled up behind him to envelope him in Reiki. James was very receptive and grateful for the Reiki energy and after two and half-hours he indicated that he had what he needed.

Bonnie and her husband thanked me, however I could tell they were disappointed that James was still panting and seemed to be in pain. I tried to explain that Reiki heals for the greatest good and we don't always know what the greatest good is. Unfortunately, that didn't seem to comfort them. I said my goodbyes and I had a wonderful feeling from James and felt the outcome would be a good one.

The next day I phoned Bonnie to see how James was doing. She said they had seen their vet and James seemed to be doing much better and thanked me for my concern.

A few months went by and one day, while out shopping, I ran into Bonnie's husband and I inquired about James's condition. He told me that after my visit, the vet had miraculously cured James of the heartworms. James is doing great and is very healthy. In fact, you would never know that he had ever been that sick!

"Isn't that amazing?" she told me. "He sure is an incredible vet!"

(This is a true story, however the names have been changed to protect those still in denial.)

About the Author: Lisa Chapman-Sorci is a member of a family of multi-generational energy workers and animal communicators. She has been showing others the way to happier, healthier lives through Reiki and Meditation for six years and is the founder of Healing Alternatives Reiki/Meditation Center in Carmichael, California. Please visit her website at www.healing-alternatives.org.

Chelsea and Quinn: A Reiki Love Story

By Julie Keefe

May 1987

Here I was, just me, just 21-years-old and moving into my first apartment. It was exciting to have a place of my own, but the long-term forecast looked pretty lonely. It was the same day that I picked out Chelsea, or maybe she picked me out. She was too old to be a kitten, but still too young to be considered full-grown. That gave us something in common. We needed each other. So

I paid the forty-dollar fee to set her free and took her home with me. Little did I know that my forty dollars would buy us an eighteen-year friendship.

May 2001

It started with watching a program about the plight of retired greyhounds. There was so much I did not know about these beautiful animals. After I did learn, I could not forget. My family and I found ourselves seriously entertaining the possibility of welcoming a retired greyhound into our home. Synchronicity supports us in unseen ways when we finally say, "yes" to what has been saying, "yes" to us. Through a chain of encouragement and assistance too complicated to remember, and within a matter of days, we received the phone number of an amazing couple in Anderson Township who place greyhounds in 'forever' (permanent) homes. Shortly thereafter, we met with them and were introduced to their greyhound, Quinn. Once you meet Quinn, there is no turning back. He worked his magic and made us fall in love with him, his toothy grin and his dancing brown eyes. We were smitten. We could not wait to adopt a greyhound just like him.

June 2004

If my cat Chelsea could talk, I think she would thank me for becoming a Reiki practitioner, especially after I received my second level attunement. She never liked me placing my hands on her, but she would sleep for hours on the spot where I had treated myself with Reiki. I believe that the Reiki I performed supported the good health she experienced at her advanced age. We have been together through eight moves into new homes, and the addition of a husband, child and greyhound to what had once been our family of two. Despite the changes and commotion, Chelsea remained flexible and constant. Although many things in this world are uncertain, I could count on the love of this cat for me, and on her love of the Reiki treatments I gave her.

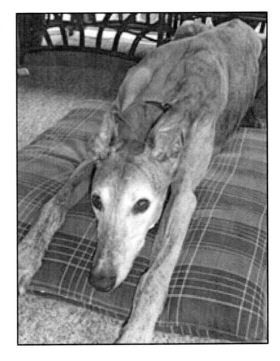

November 2005

It is news that no one wants to hear: Quinn's people learned that their beloved pet had cancer. They were distraught and confused about their options. In addition to offering them my support, it was a gift and privilege to be able to share Reiki healing with my friend, Quinn. He welcomed it, as most animals do. I felt the energy I sent flowing into Quinn, strong and clear, as he drifted off to asleep. It was a humbling experience to be a conduit on his behalf. Of course, I could make no assurances as to how Reiki would help his situation. Hopefully, it was enough to know that it would be for the highest good of all.

Less than a week later, Chelsea began her unmistakable decline. There was no question that she was ready to take her leave. With a heavy heart, but deep gratitude, I let her go. The next day, I shared with Quinn's owners the sad news of Chelsea's passing the night before. Their reply stunned me and then filled my heart and eyes to brimming; Quinn had passed the night before, as well.

He and Chelsea crossed the Rainbow Bridge together, sending a powerful message of gratitude for their forever homes and time with us. These beloved animals blessed our lives with their arrival and graced us with their peaceful passing. Looking back, I cannot help but wonder who was really giving and receiving the love that is Reiki.

About the Author: Julie Keefe and her family reside in Cincinnati, Ohio and actively support Greyhound Adoption of Greater Cincinnati. Julie lovingly offers Reiki treatments to animals and their people. Please visit her website at www.magicbeansworkshop.com.

True's Eyes

By Nancy O'Donohue

Several months ago I was having a phone conversation with my friend Lynn about things we stress and worry about. She was giving me examples of the type of things she worries about and included the statement, "I worry about whether I should have my dog's eyes taken out..." Now there's a sentence I've never heard in all my years, so I interrupted her and asked what she was talking about! Lynn explained that two years before, her six year old Basenji, True, had developed a degenerative eye condition and was gradually going blind. True had undergone extensive testing and veterinarians were unable to find any underlying cause so they attributed her condition to immune mediated disease. Tests did reveal that the degeneration in sight was the result of damage to the nerves caused by extremely high pressures in her eyes (glaucomic events). The vet felt the pressure must have been causing True discomfort, probably something like having a constant migraine. There was also extreme inflammation in both eyes causing redness and further discomfort. The vet prescribed steroids and anti-inflammatory oral medications and eye drops.

While the steroids and anti-inflammatories helped some to reduce the pressures, True continued to experience spikes in pressure which continued to damage the nerves until finally True became completely blind. At this point the vet felt that continuing with steroids was not the best course of action and recommended either removing True's eyes or giving her injections in the eyes that would ultimately deaden the mucous membrane where the pressure built. While neither treatment would heal the underlying cause of her disease or restore her sight, they would resolve the pressure issue and relieve the pain she was experiencing. Had he given the injections before True went blind, the injections would have caused blindness. Lynn chose to try the injections because she did not feel that removing the eyes was a good option. Shortly after True received the injections, I spoke with Lynn and she told me it would be some time before they would know if the injections did the job and she was concerned that while the pressure issue might be resolved, the underlying cause, i.e. the immune mediated disease, was still an issue. There was no noticeable change in True's demeanor: she was still basically a couch potato and not playful. I offered to give True long distance Reiki treatments, since she is in California and I am in Michigan.

We scheduled the first session at a time when Lynn was home with True so she could tell me how True reacted during the treatment. While I was sending Reiki to True, the word "despair" came to me very strongly. I chose not to tell Lynn this at the time because I knew it would upset her, she was doing everything she could for True and I felt confident the situation was going to improve. When I spoke with Lynn after the session, she said True had been in her usual vegetative state the entire 30 minutes. I took this as a sign she was accepting the treatment, particularly since she'd sent me a message as to how she was feeling emotionally.

Lynn also told me that the morning after the long distance session, True jumped onto the edge of Lynn's bed which she hadn't tried to do for 3-4 months because she had difficulty judging the height of the bed. Lynn took this as a good sign that her spirits were lifted and she felt better after the session. True was also more excited about going for her walk that morning, another encouraging sign.

I next gave True 30-minute sessions four days in a row while Lynn was at work. We spoke at the end of the four days and Lynn reported that the only change was that True had jumped up on Lynn's lap one day (while True normally will sit very close to be petted she does not sit on Lynn's lap) and that morning ran back for a toy as they left for their walk, something else she had never done. I was pleased because these seemed to be signs True was feeling more playful and must therefore have been feeling more physically comfortable. An interesting event was that for two days out of the four I did sessions for True, I felt pressure on my eyes! This is something I had never experienced before or after and I felt I was being gifted with feeling what True had been experiencing for the past two years. Such long-term, constant discomfort would certainly be cause for despair.

I continued giving True Reiki sessions twice a week and during that time Lynn reported subtle changes in True's behavior. In one e-mail to me she said True "seems to want to run a bit in the morning and she's not sleeping as much -- she stays awake between the time I come home and bedtime. She's also a little more cuddly and wants to be petted more. I do think she's more comfortable than she was a month ago." Later, Lynn reported she was seeing definite changes in True's behavior. True was taking more interest in her toys, sitting with Lynn more instead of in a chair across the room and hopping and skipping more than she'd ever done, like she was really excited about stuff, be it a treat or going for a walk.

A month later, the vet confirmed that the pressures in True's eyes were within normal limits and True could be taken off the steroids. True still had inflammation in the eyes for which she was to receive anti-inflammatory drops.

This was wonderful news. When I started working with True I wasn't sure what would happen, since I had never before tried long distance sessions on an animal, only on humans. I continued with the Reiki treatments and Lynn has reported the redness caused by inflammation in True's eyes is reduced and she continues to be more playful and alert. True's response to the treatments gave me the confidence to try long distance sessions on many other animals, and all have had positive results!

I will continue to give True sessions every other week to maintain the excellent progress that has been made so far. The reward in knowing an animal who was in pain and seems to be now pain-free is really immeasurable.

About the author: Nancy O'Donohue is a Reiki Level III Master/Teacher in Fennville, Michigan who treats humans, pets and horses in southwestern Michigan. Please visit her website at www.LakeshoreHealing.com.

Gizmo's Amazing Recovery from Cancer

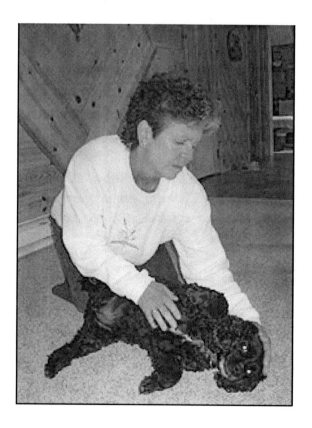

By Diane Hedges

I have been a Reiki practitioner for just over a year now, and my focus has been on Reiki for animals. Sometimes doubt would creep in, and I would wonder if I was really helping them. Then I had an experience that removed all my doubt.

My Dog Gizmo became ill (coughing, lethargy), so I took her to the vet. She got a complete physical, including blood work and X-rays. The X-rays showed two spots on her lungs, and the initial diagnosis was lung cancer, but as a precautionary measure the films were sent to a doctor at Michigan State University, an excellent college of veterinary medicine. The results from their doctor confirmed "primary lung cancer."

Even before the results came back I began doing 15 to 20 minutes of Reiki on Gizmo each day (and also put her on an all-natural immunity booster and Omega 3 fatty acids), and I continued for two months until she went back to the doctor for follow-up X-rays. This second set of films showed that one of the two spots had completely disappeared, and the second was smaller. There was celebrating at our house that day!

I continued with the intensive Reiki, and a month later she went back in for more X-rays. You can imagine our joy when they showed totally clear lungs!

The head doctor at our vet clinic was skeptical, so she took abdominal X-rays, thinking to find cancer there, and guess what – NOTHING on the films!

Today Gizmo is a happy, healthy dog who just celebrated her eighth birthday. She still begs for her Reiki sessions, and I thank God every day for my dog's life and for the beautiful gift He has given me.

About the Author: Diane Hedges is a Reiki II Practitioner in Gladwin, Michigan. She can be contacted at dianekhedges@aol.com.

Saving Sparky

By Heather St. Giles

Over 5 years ago our dog, a lab-mix named Sparky, was chasing a deer at night when he suffered a very grave injury falling off of an embankment. He immediately suffered great pain and confusion; he couldn't walk due to the paralysis of his rear limbs. By morning, he had both bowel and bladder incontinence. We took him to his vet, who diagnosed a spinal cord injury. He gave a very guarded prognosis if we followed up with an MRI and emergency neurosurgeon to relieve the pressure from the bulging disk in his back. If we didn't, the vet said it was only merciful to put him down. My son was heartbroken; we agreed we couldn't put him down immediately, so we took the dog home.

We had just moved into our condominium, and we didn't know anybody in town. I didn't have the resources to obtain the advanced care for my dog, so we just waited to see if he could recover. After 2 weeks, the dog was so miserable, we arranged for a vet to come to our house and perform the euthanasia procedure on Halloween. It was a sad decision, but the right thing to do.

A friendly neighbor saw us on our walkway taking care of our inert dog while walking his dog. When he asked what was wrong with our dog, we told him our sad story. An hour later, the neighbors' wife stopped by, introduced herself as Ellen, and asked if she could help Sparky with Reiki. I was a bit surprised, we didn't know about Ellen or Reiki, but I had no hesitation about letting the woman try and help the stricken animal. The vet was coming in less than 2 days - what did we have to lose? Ellen sat and knelt on the walkway beside the dog, and gently petted him. The dog relaxed visibly in Ellen's presence, so we watched, then gave them a little space and time, such as the sidewalk allowed. After a half hour or so, she stood up, petted Sparky a final time, wished us good luck, and wished Sparky a speedy recovery. We smiled, nodded, but didn't expect a thing from our friendly neighbor and offbeat encounter.

However, to our amazement, within an hour Sparky perked up, then tried to get up! And an hour later, he staggered to his feet! We calmed him, but by morning he had regained bowel and bladder continence, and began to walk later that day. He recovered steadily over the next 2 weeks, much to our delight. Needless to say, we cancelled the vet's appointment. Ellen saw him once more, which seemed to complete the healing process. Sparky is still with us today, and is 11 years old now. Ellen still enjoys visiting with Sparky while walking in the neighborhood. We are very, very grateful to Ellen for her healing Reiki that saved our dog.

About the Practitioner: Ellen has been practicing Reiki for over ten years. She studied under Kathleen Prasad and Frans Stiene. She has a great love for all animals, and offers Reiki to every kind, from companion animals to insects. She volunteers at The Marin Humane Society and BrightHaven. She can be reached at allcreaturesreiki@yahoo.com.

A Message from Belle

By Nancy O'Donohue

Belle is a beautiful 7-year old Golden Retriever/Pyrenese mix adopted from the Humane Society who turned out to have allergies resulting in fur loss and rashes. Her human caretaker, Marty, has worked with their veterinarian trying different medications and variations in diet which have helped for awhile, but the loss of fur and rashes always returned. Marty felt Reiki might help and called me.

When I met with Belle, she started out hesitant as to whom I was and what I was going to do so she stayed close to Marty. Once I started offering her Reiki, she came over and smelled my hands [a frequent response as animals can feel the energy coming from them] and lay down beside me. She put her head on my hand and was very receptive to the energy, and a few times rolled onto her back as if to show me the bare spots on her belly.

After about 10 minutes I asked her if there was anything she wanted to tell me; Belle immediately got up and walked into the kitchen and stuck her nose into an empty glass bowl on the floor! It was the cat's bowl of canned pet milk which Marty usually shoos Belle away from but we gave her some right then and there. Then Belle returned to the floor and let me continue giving her Reiki. Animals are very sensitive and intuitive and often know what they need, so asking them is an important part of the treatment process. But Belle's answer to my question was by far the most interesting response I've ever received.

Since Belle's Reiki session [and the inclusion of dairy in her diet], Belle has had more energy, her fur started growing back and her rashes are minimal. Energy healing strengthens the body's immune system, thereby providing a line of defense against allergic reactions. I also referred Belle's family to a holistic vet who practices Nambrudiped's Allergy Elimination Technique [NAET], a powerful holistic method for eliminating the root cause of allergies. As energy healing is a complementary therapy, I always encourage clients to pursue all possible veterinary treatments for a well-rounded approach to healing.

About the Author: Nancy O'Donohue is a Reiki Level III Master/Teacher who treats humans, pets and horses in southwestern Michigan. Please visit her website at www.LakeshoreHealing.com.

Max-a-Million

By John Sawyer

I first met Max in March of 2006. I had just begun offering Reiki to the animals at Animals In Distress http://www. animalsindistress-pa.org in Coopersburg, PA near where I work. The staff at the shelter was open to Reiki as the kennel manager had been attuned to Reiki Level 1 some years earlier, but they weren't too sure what to do with Reiki and me. They chose two dogs for me to start with: Amigo and Max. Both had been recently diagnosed with lymphosarcoma. Amigo is a Husky-Chow mix who has been at the shelter for a number of years. Max was a Scottish Terrier, all black and full of energy. Max was about 5 years old and had a heart condition aside from his new illness. The heart condition made it more difficult to treat him. Amigo was undergoing the standard chemotherapy regimen specified by the vets working with AID, however, it was felt that Max' heart could not take the effects of the same drug so he was put on a different less potent drug. He had just begun his treatments when I met him.

At the first session, one of the kennel staff held Max' leash while I offered him Reiki. He seemed more interested in investigating the room we were in and darted here and there. At one point, Lori reached down to adjust his leash and gasped, looking at me horrified. I said, "What's wrong?" She said, "Feel his neck!" I did so and felt quite a number of large lumps all around Max' neck. If I hadn't known better, I'd have thought he'd visited the next-door golf course and swallowed a bucket of balls! I continued to offer him Reiki and Max continued unfazed by our discovery of his condition. After about 20 minutes, Max stopped drawing energy from me and I told Lori he was through for the day. Lori was unfamiliar with Reiki and with me and gave me a sort of "Okay, I'll take your word for it" look. I found out the following week that the lumps in Max' neck had completely disappeared 48 hours later. No one at the shelter was quite ready to attribute that to Reiki, but it was a definite step in the right direction.

I continued to visit Max over the next several weeks and Lori always sat with us and kept Max' leash. She asked me questions about what I was doing and what Reiki was about. I had arranged to teach a class at AID for the interested kennel staff and Lori was looking forward to that. I don't think she really knew anything was going on in terms of energy between Max and me until one day Max was being his usual busy self and suddenly stopped still, head up, ears cocked and fully alert. At that moment, I felt a surge of energy and Lori, much to her surprise, said she felt a wave of heat jump from Max to her. Max stayed still for about 30 seconds, and then resumed his exploration of the room. Lori was quite surprised by the experience, but from then on knew that there was something more to this Reiki stuff than she had thought previously.

Max finished his course of chemotherapy and for several months seemed to be doing well. Later that summer, however, a visit to the vet showed that the cancer had returned. The vets predicted he had a few months left and put him on a different medication. I continued to see Max every week and gave him healing attunements every three weeks or so as well as his regular Reiki sessions. He continued to be the little ball of energy I had come to know.

In mid-December Max took a turn for the worse. The vets decided to try aggressive chemotherapy to turn him around. Unfortunately, the drug took such a toll on him that they stopped the treatments after the second round. Max seemed to age several years in the space of a few weeks. He began losing hair and lost his ability to jump up on things. I wasn't able to see him for several weeks during the holidays due to number of factors, but began regular sessions with him again in January. The first session, he was obviously weak and tired. The spark had gone out of him. The following week, however, he looked better and was more interested in investigating his surroundings. There was a calmness about him now, not the frenetic energy I was used to. He seemed wiser somehow and more peaceful.

At what was to be my last session with Max we had a wonderful time playing with a tug toy. Max seemed happy and peaceful and I left with a good feeling about the time I'd spent with him. Three days later he made his transition after spending a day with one of the kennel staff who had been taking him to her house for regular visits. Looking back, I can see that he was saying goodbye to his friends and had made his decision to return home to Source energy. I know that Reiki helped him to make that transition easily and on his own terms. He is fully healed in spirit and is now pure positive energy. He taught me a great deal and I am honored to have known him.

About the Author: John Sawyer is a software engineer and Reiki Master who has been owned by 10 dogs over the past 17 years. Through those years, he and his wife, Donna, have dealt with a number of canine health crises which led them through the mainstream veterinary field to alternative health care modalities including acupuncture and Reiki. John took Reiki Level 1 in 1994 and experimented with applying the Reiki techniques to caring for his dogs, eventually taking Level 2 before becoming a Master in 2004. He is currently building his animal Reiki practice and offering Reiki training to local shelters and other animal workers in the Lehigh Valley area of Eastern PA. Please visit his website at www.critterreiki.com or you can contact him at john@critterreiki.com.

Brutus and Me

By Beth Lowell

I don't know what happened to me there, in Brutus' kitchen. Brutus was wagging his tail and doing an excited dance, expecting to go for a walk. I could feel the pressure rise in my chest. My lips turned numb. I couldn't catch my breath and if I'd had hackles, they would have been rising. Brutus was now confused. His ears went down and he looked at me funny.

A large black dog of unknown descent, Brutus had been adopted by Eric and Jennifer five years earlier after he was surrendered due to "some issues" with an uncle in the family. This had been Brutus' last chance at a home. Powerfully built with a square head and only the faintest touch of dark brown fur that lined his underside, he had not been a welcome addition to the neighborhood. People were scared of him.

As his new pet sitter, I met him the day after he came home. I was sitting in the kitchen when he came down from upstairs. He thought I belonged there. We were pals from the start. I worked hard with him to keep him calm on walks; he became crazed at the sight of passing cars, and other dogs were also a challenge. Eric and Jennifer took him to special classes for feisty dogs where he made enormous strides, but he remained territorial and Eric and Jennifer were reluctant to introduce him to another pet sitter.

I walked Brutus over the years, off and on, through layoffs, new jobs and a baby. He mellowed and the neighbors even allowed him to play with their dog. All was right with the world.

And then one day as I put on his gentle leader, just as I always did, he bared his teeth at me. I didn't register what was happening. I had never seen Brutus bare his teeth at me before. In fact, although I'd seen him get riled up over a passing UPS truck, I don't recall ever seeing him bare his teeth. I put on his gentle leader and we went for a walk. I returned later that day to feed him dinner and take him out again. This time, I noticed the teeth and realized that this was a communication aimed at me.

I called Jennifer later and explained what had happened. I thought maybe Brutus wasn't feeling well, or had injured his snout where the strap of the gentle leader lay against his skin. She wasn't aware of anything wrong with Brutus, and she put the head halter on him right then without a problem. I asked her if I could stop by while she was home to practice with the gentle leader to make sure he was okay with it. She agreed, and when I went over the next day I put the gentle leader on without a problem. Everything was fine.

Jennifer laughed and said "Eric said he knew there'd be no problem. When I asked him how he knew that, he said, 'Brutus always pulls through in the end, when his back's up against the wall.' And I told Brutus he better shape up or he was done for."

I wanted to be sure everything went well before my next visit with Brutus. I started a daily practice of meditation. I balanced my chakras. I meditated on developing fearlessness, faith and trust. I visualized sending Brutus a healing light from my heart to his.

So now, here I was, back in the kitchen, in the middle of a panic attack, exacerbated by the sight of a very large black dog who had turned inexplicably into a threatening stranger. While he was not displaying any aggression whatsoever, my panic level continued to rise. He slunk down. I tried to order Brutus to sit but my voice came out high and uneven. He sat. I pleaded with him to stay. I backed out of the kitchen feeling as though my head would pop off and gently closed the door behind me. My fingers rattled as I turned the key in the lock. I was too shaken up to think about Reiki.

I called Jennifer to let her know that I had not taken Brutus out. I felt foolish telling her I'd had a panic attack, and like I'd somehow let her, Eric and Brutus down and this added to my anxiety. Lamely I told her that his baring his teeth must have affected me more deeply than I'd realized. She was very understanding, yet I could picture her
and her husband having a conversation about me, about how I must have come unhinged. I told her I'd call her when I figured out a plan for coming back.

I procrastinated. My schedule had become too full, as it often does during vacation months. I barely had time for a shower, let alone the peace and quiet I needed to formulate a plan. My friends told me to give up Brutus as a client.

I mentioned what had happened to me in my animal Reiki class. No one else in class seemed to have an issue like mine. Though no one said anything, I thought the class probably thought I was nutty too. I stopped talking about it at class. I asked members of my Animal Reiki Yahoo group for help. It couldn't hurt, I thought.

Jennifer called to see how I was doing and I felt guilty for avoiding her. I had to tell her something. I took a leap. I told her about Reiki and my aspirations for becoming an animal Reiki practitioner. I told her that Reiki was a Japanese healing technique developed for people that worked on body, mind and spirit and that it was commonly used in hospitals, especially for pain management in cancer patients. Now, it was being used to help animals too. I asked if I could come and give Brutus a Reiki treatment from the deck. She agreed.

I told her that I would come to the door and give Brutus a treat to say hello and then I would close the door, sit on the deck and offer Reiki. I would let her know when I was finished. When I sat on the deck I felt the Reiki almost immediately, flowing strongly from my arms. The landscapers were next door and oddly enough the sound of the mowers and leaf blowers was not distracting. It became a comforting white noise to me. I imagined briefly the landscapers too, wondering if I was crazy, as I sat placidly amid the din, in the sunshine on the floor of the deck with my palms up. After a half hour, the tingling in my arms subsided. I went to the door and gave Brutus another treat. Still wary, I pushed Kathleen Prasad's brochure through the door because I knew Jennifer would probably have more questions about Reiki. I didn't yet have a brochure of my own.

I scheduled another Reiki session for the following week, but it was raining so I postponed. I was relieved for the reprieve. I had little hope for next week's session. I had felt the Reiki flow, but Jennifer had not seen Brutus respond in any particular way. Although I knew I was supposed to assume that Reiki went where it was supposed to go, I was having my doubts. I started to think that maybe I was crazy after all. I wondered how long Jennifer would put up with my plan. I had a feeling it would be a long process.

I told Jennifer I would sit on the deck again. She wanted to leave the back door open so Brutus would know I was there. I wasn't ready to see Brutus. I didn't say anything. When I got to the house on that brilliant Tuesday morning I felt defeated before I started. My schedule was busier than I had expected it to be. I was trying to get ready for vacation. I just wanted this to be over. As I pulled into the driveway I saw the newspaper still lying there, and the dry cleaning that had been delivered. Almost on autopilot, I retrieved the paper and collected the dry cleaning. It occurred to me that if I carried these things into the house as I normally would, perhaps I could actually get into the house this time, if just for a moment. I opened the door and Brutus came to greet me. I gave him a cheerful greeting despite the queasy feeling that had started to come over me. I was determined to get past the threshold. I carried the paper and clothing in and said hello to Jennifer.

We exchanged a few pleasantries and then Jennifer said, "I was telling my mom about Reiki. She was in the hospital last year with cancer. She was lucky not to have to undergo extensive treatment, but she knew a lot of people there who had gotten Reiki as a complement to chemo and radiation." This was more than I could have hoped for. Encouraged by this, but still wary I shared some stories of Reiki miracles that I and other members of the class had experienced. Instead of the polite disinterest I half expected, Jennifer said she thought it was really cool.

I ended up sitting at the kitchen table, where I'd first met Brutus, and offered him Reiki. He wandered between me and Jennifer and the baby but eventually settled down on his side. He let out a huge sigh. After a while he rose and pushed into me and I positioned my hands along his torso. He turned and licked my hands. After the Reiki stopped flowing, I thanked Brutus. Jennifer was amazed by his reaction. She said she had never seen him settle down so deeply. And after I left, he didn't even bark at the mail truck.

I've been back to see Brutus, both for Reiki and for walks. I came away from this experience with a renewed faith in Reiki and in myself. I'll never know why Brutus did what he did or why I reacted so strongly but it doesn't really matter. I'll never take our relationship for granted, but I know that whatever hiccup in it occurred has been
expelled. This experience showed me the true healing essence of Reiki – both for the recipient and for the practitioner.

About the Author: Beth Lowell is a dog lover-owner-walker-writer and artist who has recently expanded her horizons into the world of Animal Reiki. She is looking forward to the journey! You can contact Beth at beth@animalslovereiki.com or visit her website at www.animalslovereiki.com.

Part 3:
Reiki for Horses

Reiki for Princess and Koko

By Susan Garrioch

This is a story about a wonderful horse called Princess and her buddy Koko. Princess produced many wonderful, friendly foals for me. Koko, who is presently 22 years old, has been her friend for many years.

I sold Princess about three years ago, to what I had thought was a good home. All was well until I received a dreaded phone call last December 2005, to say she had injured her eye and the people could no longer care for her and her current foal. Without even going to see them I arranged for them to be picked up, and was shocked by what I found. Princess' left eye was so infected that the eyeball had shrunk and receded back into the socket.

After many months of care I moved Princess to be with her buddy Koko. It was instant friendship again and the two are still inseparable. Princess had her eye removed under the watchful supervision of Koko who insisted that she remain by her side during the procedure. The surgery went well and that evening I went to see them in their pasture and for the first time asked Princess if she would like some Reiki. I was astonished at the results- you have to remember that I am new to the wonders of Reiki. Princess had been traumatized to the point that she had become vicious sometimes, due to pain, but as soon I offered Reiki she has never looked back. I offered Reiki to Princess daily for about a month and now offer it about twice a week or more if she wants it. She has turned into a "Reiki Junkie" and isn't happy walking in from the field unless I have my hand on her neck.

Koko, who has cancer and is very arthritic, had shown no interest in Reiki until about a week after Princess had her surgery. Koko was looking at me and so I asked her if she would like some Reiki. Koko stood looking at me and from a distance, I offered her Reiki. After about five minutes she started to sway from side to side and she buckled at the knees but did not lie down. The reaction she had was scary but I persisted as long as she wanted to accept what

I was offering. At the end of the treatment she stretched, as I have never seen her do before, arched her back and then looked at me and walked off. Koko will now step between Princess and myself to get some Reiki when she feels she needs it. I have had Koko since she was three years old, and we have formed a special bond, which has been enhanced thanks to Reiki.

I can't express the feeling I have being alone with my two best friends and being able to offer them something so simple as Reiki yet so powerful. I have had similar occurrences with hummingbirds who seem to follow me wherever I go, especially when I am offering Reiki.

About the Author: Susan resides in Elgin, Ontario, Canada. She completed Level 2 in spring of 2007. She has always been attracted to animals, especially horses and dogs, and finds Reiki to be the link she was missing when communicating with her horses. She can be reached at s_garrioch@yahoo.com.

Rescuing Pawnee

By Susan Mountjoy

I first met my horse 2 years ago when he came limping down my long driveway. I live on a horse-boarding farm and at first I thought one of the horses had escaped, but this was an Appaloosa I'd never seen before. He was obviously old and sick and starving, but underneath the dirt and scars was a beautiful red roan coat with mahogany spots. And his eyes - despite his suffering he looked at me through these dark serene eyes as though he were saying, "I finally found you." He pressed his head against me and stood still for the longest time while I rubbed his ears. I named him Pawnee.

Tire marks and hoof prints at the top of the top of the driveway showed a truck and trailer had pulled up, left him and drove away. I never learned who it was but at least he found his way to me. We began our healing journey together by having the vet visit. At first the vet agreed the horse was old, but after examining his teeth he said he was only 8 or 9. He had horrific burns on one hip, whip marks, hundreds of crusted sores and lesions, a recent deep slash on his shoulder the vet was able to stitch up. He had some type of severe injury to his neck muscles and wasn't able to graze without spreading his legs apart, like a giraffe.

Pawnee could only eat mash at first, slowly graduating to senior horse feed and then to pasture grass. I made him soft horse muffins with lots of molasses and he did a little dance whenever he saw me coming with them. No matter what procedure he had to endure he was always still and calm. After one year I rode him and he did beautifully. But even though his physical problems had improved I knew memories still bothered him - men with dark beards...old blue pickup trucks...loud voices. I knew about Reiki but I thought it was just for people. Then I read about Kathleen's book, 'Animal Reiki', and immediately ordered it. The day it came I opened it to a random page and said out loud, 'I'm going to do this for Pawnee!' I searched everywhere for a Reiki teacher locally and finally found one. After completing Reiki 1 I gave Pawnee a

treatment. He was very receptive and was relaxed and yawning. 3 weeks later I took Reiki 2 and what a difference! I stood at the far end of the field Pawnee was in and did my 1st distant treatment. He turned around and looked at me, then began trotting down the hill and inspected my hands thoroughly. What a difference level 2 made! He just soaked it up, pulling huge amounts, but there was still that aura about him, a feeling as though he was still waiting for something bad to happen to him...as if his new life was just too good to be true.

A month after I began giving Pawnee level 2 treatments we had quite the experience. What began as a "routine" session turned into anything but that. A few minutes into the treatment he began pulling incredible amounts of Reiki...then he started to stiffen and back up, as if he were very frightened. He looked at me almost pleadingly and began to cough and hack horribly. It truly frightened me! I wanted to run and call the vet but didn't want to leave him. His head hung down while he gagged and coughed and I put my hands back on him to try and comfort him. Immediately I had a sensation of horrible fear and despair, almost electrifying. At the time I thought it was my fear of his sudden condition, but now I know it was HIS fear coming out. I believe the coughing and choking was a healing reaction. It suddenly stopped and he stood quietly, eyes and nose running. Then he took a HUGE breath and let it out, looking at me as if to say, "Well, that's over with!"

And it is. Today Pawnee is at his proper weight, terribly spoiled and very, very happy. He likes to pull peoples' hats off and run away with them. He pulls the farrier's tools out of his back pockets and drops them. A sheriff's deputy stopped to visit him and he offered Pawnee a lifesaver in his palm. Instead of taking it, Pawnee instead yanked the entire roll of Life Savers from his other hand and galloped off, eating it, paper and all. He loves baths - the more suds the better. He adores children and helps them learn to ride. His best friend is a little Native American girl who visits often and brings peppermint sticks and gingersnaps for him. They have a game they love to play - she sticks her tongue out him and HE sticks HIS tongue out at her! This goes on and on until she usually falls down on the grass laughing. People don't believe this until they see the photo of them together. What a pair!

Pawnee doesn't mind bearded men any longer, or old blue pickups. He's laid-back and serene. He's found his forever home and I've gained a forever friend. It was a fortuitous day that he came down my driveway. Thank you, Reiki.

About the Author: Susan Mountjoy lives on a horse farm in the beautiful Rocky Mountains of Colorado. She is a Reiki Level 2 healer and is working on building her practice, 'Kindred Spirit Animal Reiki'. She volunteers at local animal shelters and also offers Reiki to law enforcement canines. She says, "Kathleen's outstanding course has had a phenomenal effect on my Reiki practice." You can contact Susan at bostonbean46@hotmail.com.

Reiki and Recovery:
The Comeback of "Marvelous" Max

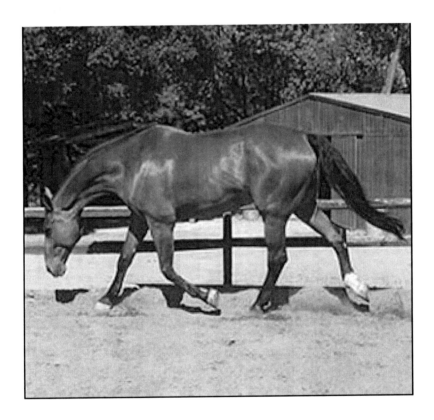

By Kathleen Prasad

Originally published in *Natural Horse Talk Magazine*, Sept.-Oct. 2005, Volume 1, Issue 5.

I first began treating Max, or Marvelous, as he is known in the show world, with Reiki in March of 2005. It was at that time that my trainer, Alison, acquired him from a friend and dressage trainer. Little did I know the many obstacles Max had overcome in order to get to this turning point in his life. I only knew that he was extremely sensitive and responsive to energy, and therefore to the Reiki I offered. And so our relationship began, composed of weekly Reiki sessions and occasional pats during the week when I would see him out and about with Alison.

The first Reiki treatment I gave Max was interesting. I must admit that doing Reiki on a horse whose legs were as tall as my chest was a bit intimidating. But as soon as I entered his stall and asked for his permission to begin the treatment, he put his gigantic nose against my chest. He slowly began to take the edge of my t-shirt into his mouth to suck on. He really was like a gigantic puppy dog! As I began the treatment, I immediately sensed a great anxiety from him. To me as a practitioner of Reiki, this feels like tightness in my chest. Usually it will dissipate by the end of the treatment, as Reiki helps to release the feeling, bringing emotional healing to the animal.

Sure enough, as I moved my hands over his body, the feeling of anxiety lessened. Max seemed to appreciate hands-on Reiki, so I began the treatment with my hands lightly at his shoulders, and progressed down his body on either side, ending on his hind legs. As I put my hands over his hind legs, he picked each leg up and stretched them high into the air and backward. I would later discover the difficulties he had faced regarding those legs. As I finished the treatment, Max's head had dropped, his lower lip hanging loosely in relaxation. He barely stirred as I thanked him and left the stall. He was deeply into what I call "Reiki land," a common state of deep peace and repose induced by a Reiki treatment.

Max is an 11 year old Dutch Warm blood, 18.2 hands in height. He was born in Holland, where he was destined for Grand Prix dressage, the very highest level of dressage skill in the world. Although he is gigantic, he is extremely well-proportioned and a wonderful mover. When Max was 5, Alison's friend went to Europe looking for a dressage horse to train to the Grand Prix level. She fell in love with him and imported him to California. She trained him in dressage for 5 years. In the beginning, Max was wonderful. He was fine in the basics of dressage, but as the difficulty of the upper levels progressed, Max began to refuse to work. The intense collection that was required at these levels was very difficult, and Max just didn't want to do it. He began to get anxious: he would threaten to rear and just get "stuck". Because he is so enormous, it was extremely intimidating. If the issue was forced, things began to escalate even further. Eventually, his person decided that it was hard enough to train a willing horse to do Grand Prix, and she just didn't want to fight with him.

So, Max's person began to ask the question, "What else?" She thought perhaps he could be a jumper. And so, she began to try him over a few jumps. It was winter and he had just begun to jump, when he got scratches on his lower legs. This kind of injury is very common in horses, especially in wintertime, but with Max, the scratches didn't heal but only got worse. They worsened into a bacterial infection that spiraled out of control. Overnight, his back legs swelled to 3 times their normal size. He was given a strong dose of antibiotics, but the wrong type of antibiotics, so the infection continued to grow in severity. Pretty soon he had a full blown systemic infection, lymphangitis, and a 104 degree fever. He was hospitalized for 10 days, where he was finally given the correct antibiotic and began to recover. After his return home, he was given stall rest and slowly he recovered. Finally, his person decided it was time to find him the right home where he would be happy in his work.

This is where Alison came into the picture. In late January, she first met Max when looking for a horse for some clients. Over the next couple of months, she visited Max several times. Although Max was officially for sale, his person had no desire to let go of him for just "any person." She wanted the right home and trainer for this special horse. After several interested parties just weren't "perfect", she decided she'd rather give him to the right home than sell him to the wrong one. She had known Alison for many years: Alison used to ride with her daughter when they were young. She knew what kind of training program Alison had, and her talent with horses. So, she asked Alison if she would take him.

By now it was March and Max had been basically out of work for 4 months. He really had no muscle and needed to rebuild his strength. Alison began riding him lightly but regularly to bring him back into shape very gradually. For 6 weeks, she continued to keep tight standing wraps on him all the time, except when riding. She was gradually able to wean him off these wraps as his legs resumed their normal size.

I continued regular Reiki treatments for Max from March through the present. As the months passed, I felt great improvement in his energetic balance. His behavior too, was different. The anxiety that had plagued him for so long in training was gone. He expressed a new happiness and interest in people, nickering at anyone who walked by. He would gently grab people's clothing or hats to get their attention. With the summer months in full swing, he was now able to be turned out in a large, grassy field to run and play. He moved to an outdoor paddock, out of the barn where he had lived all winter, and loved his new home. As he learned to jump competently, his confidence increased and personality emerged. He began to show an increasingly affectionate side: licking the sides of people's faces, playing with people's hair, and answering to anyone who called his name.

He began to like receiving Reiki treatments in a specific way: As I enter his paddock, he comes and greets me, pushing his nose into my chest and licking my palms or carefully pulling my hat off my head. Once I ask permission and begin the Reiki treatment, he walks into his 3 sided shelter and settles in for a nap. Each time, his head drops all the way to the ground as he yawns several times. He occasionally sways so much in his sleep that it looks like his knees are about to buckle! Respectfully, I keep the distance between us, treating him from about 15 feet away. Occasionally, he wakes up long enough to arch his back like a cat stretching or to lift his back legs into the air.

At the end of the treatment, he approaches me again and breathes deeply into my chest, before walking away and resuming his horsey activities (grazing, visiting neighboring horses, etc.). It is a lovely pattern of treatment that we both enjoy. He knows why I'm there and appreciates the healing energy, and I let him choose to receive the treatment exactly as he is comfortable to receive it.

In addition to Reiki, Max is receiving chiropractic every other month. His chiropractor says he's never been better! He also is receiving regular massage and his masseuse reports that he is stronger each time. The more fit he is, the happier he is: many days he absolutely can't wait to get to the next jump.

Another piece of this puzzle is what I call the "kid" factor. Max is now being regularly ridden by a very talented 12 year old. Although when she rides him she is in serious training, with goals to accomplish, she is also having a great time: having fun! This attitude of "playtime" rather than "work time" is, I think, also a big factor in Max's enthusiasm and joy for his new career.

So what is in Max's future? He has come back from a serious illness and faced a change of "person" and training discipline. He has faced his new life and new challenges with humor, grace and courage. With the right combination of patient training, holistic healing, and awesome kids, I see Max's future as very bright!

Healing Your Horse With Reiki

By Kathleen Prasad

Originally published in *Equine Wellness Magazine*, September/ October 2007

I happened to be at the barn one day to visit another horse, when I walked by a stall and was shocked by a distraught mare literally writhing in colic pain. Apparently, the cost of surgery was too high, so the horse's person had decided to "give her one night" to see if she could heal on her own; otherwise, she was to be put down the following morning.

With permission, I took the mare out of her stall and into the arena where she could move around a bit more easily. I cradled her head with both hands as she leaned heavily and miserably on my shoulder. She was unable to stand still because of her discomfort, so we walked together. I felt the Reiki pulsing through my hands, and knew that even though they were on her head, the energy would flow like a magnet to where it was most needed. That is the nature of Reiki. After about 20 minutes, the mare gave a huge sigh and was able to stand quietly. She then passed quite a bit of gas and had a large bowel movement. She clearly felt much better and I carefully led her back to her stall and left her to rest. The next morning, she was back to her old self.

How can Reiki help horses?

Reiki can help maintain your horse's health, speed healing of illness and injuries, and even ease the transition between life and death. Reiki is ideal for use with horses because it is easy to learn and use, is gentle and noninvasive, and yet can powerfully address any health issue a horse may face. Because the nature of Reiki is to create and support energetic balance, it can do no harm and can be used safely on its own or as a wonderful complement to other healing therapies, both allopathic and holistic.

Horses love Reiki because they are inherently sensitive and energetic beings who understand its nature. Reiki is a new and special way to deepen our interspecies bond and horses especially appreciate connecting with humans energetically. Reiki also has an irresistibly relaxing nature that just feels good!

Let your equine partner choose

Reiki is different from most other holistic therapies in that it relies on the willing participation of the horse for success. The practitioner "offers" Reiki to the horse in a flexible way, without forcing the treatment and without expectations of the way the session will unfold. Horses are very sensitive and wise to energetic frequencies and will immediately understand the nature of the healing you are offering. Commonly, a horse will come forward and put his nose into your hands as soon as you begin. He will then choose to take Reiki in the way he needs most.

Hint

Some horses will actually come and place the areas of their bodies that need healing into your hands. Others prefer to receive the treatment from several feet away.

Normally, a Reiki treatment will consist of a combination of hands-on and hands-off, depending on the comfort and preference of the horse. In rare cases, your horse may choose not to receive a treatment on a particular day; if that happens, try again another time. You will know your horse is open to the treatment by signs of rest and relaxation: licking and chewing, frequent yawning and deep sighs, and/or falling asleep. The average Reiki treatment lasts from 30 to 60 minutes, and ends when the horse wakes up from his "Reiki nap" and moves away. Most horses will even say "thank you" by putting their heads into your hands or nuzzling you before they leave.

My horse Kodiak is a very healthy and hearty young paint who loves Reiki. I often offer it to him while he is relaxing in the pasture. I begin by asking permission and just "offering" the energy in his direction. Usually he will come over and put his head in my hands for a few moments, giving a sigh or yawn as he relaxes. After a few minutes, he will often turn and graze or nap several feet away from me. He prefers to receive a short but intense treatment that is usually done after only ten to 15 minutes. He shows me he's had enough by rousing himself from his doze, coming over and nudging me gently as if to say, "thank you," then walking purposefully away.

Getting started

Although many holistic veterinarians around the world use Reiki to help heal their patients, its use is not yet widespread in the veterinary community. The great thing is that anyone who has the desire can learn Reiki to help improve and support their horse's healing and well-being. It is a very effective yet gentle healing system that animals appreciate and enjoy at all stages of life. To get started, find a practitioner in your area and get a treatment. Once you've experienced Reiki's relaxing effects and powerful healing benefits for yourself, you will be anxious to take a course and learn to share this gift with the horses in your life.

Tips for success

1. Offer the energy; don't send it.
2. Allow the horse to move freely in the treatment space.

3. Try to let go of your expectations about what will happen: Reiki always works for the horse's highest good.

Reiki in action

He was an off-the-track thoroughbred who was clearly unhappy in his stall. Extremely nervous and high-strung, he had trouble getting along with other horses and would sometimes run himself ragged in the pasture. One day, he began to kick his stall walls over and over again. People walking by would bark, "knock it off!" but other than that, no attention was paid to him. I was concerned he might hurt himself so I left my own horse, walked to his stall window and peered in. I quietly asked, "Would you like some Reiki, sweetheart?" He immediately stopped kicking and looked directly at me. I took this to mean "yes" and began to offer him Reiki from outside the stall.

He immediately went over to the corner of his stall, lowered his head, and began licking and chewing. Within a few minutes, his head had dropped and he was sleeping soundly. I quietly walked away, ending the treatment after only a few minutes. Later that day, I alerted my trainer to his previous distress and the Reiki I had given. The next day, my trainer informed me that not only had he stopped kicking the walls, but that he had literally slept in the corner of the stall the whole previous afternoon, night and most of the morning, only rousing himself to eat. I assured her this was a good thing, as body and mind heal themselves best when we are at our most relaxed.

Part 4:
Reiki for Wild Creatures

The Visit

By Kathleen Prasad

I'll never forget that evening. It began like any other, my husband driving us along a local road to a restaurant in Mill Valley, as we had done many times before. As we approached the downtown area, the road narrows and there is a steep hill with many trees and bushes on one side. It was dark, so all the cars had their lights on. As we approached a curve in the road, I noticed something in the headlights of the oncoming car. As our car approached the other car, which had slowed down, it was clear that it was in the process of rolling over something. To my horror, it was a deer, a young buck with 2 straight horns sticking about 4 inches up off the top of his head. In that split second when I realized what I was looking at, I also processed the fact that the deer had his head tilted back and was looking straight into our car and directly into my eyes! I screamed and my hands flew to my eyes, to try to undo the horror I had seen. As we slowly passed by the scene, my husband clearly spoke to me, "Do Reiki for his spirit, he needs you."

Ah, yes, Reiki! Even I had forgotten it in that terrible moment! I began sending Reiki immediately to the scene, the situation, the spirit of the deer, the transition (that it was quick) and also to my husband's and my own wounded hearts. My eyes felt sealed shut, and my hands felt as if they began to radiate heat many feet out from my physical body. Emotionally, I felt a sudden confusion and bewilderment from the deer. I wasn't sure the deer knew that he had been hit, or even that he was making his transition. It was as if his spirit still stood in the road, transfixed and wide-eyed, not able to move on. I immediately began to send affirmations of "clarity" and "peace" to the deer's spirit, and imagined that he could easily and quickly travel to the light. After a few moments, the heat in my hands and emotions within my heart began to subside: it had been a very quick, but very intense Reiki treatment!

Somehow, my husband and I were able to collect ourselves and participate in the dinner (which was my sister's 30th birthday). On our drive home, we again discussed the terrible scene (of which all traces had been removed as we drove by again). I asked my husband, as we drove home, "Why does it seem that I'm always a witness to wild animals losing their lives to cars? It's like I'm always at the wrong place at the wrong time." My husband replied, "Or are you at the just the right place?" I pondered this as we continued our trip home. Yes, I knew that sometimes, when we open ourselves to become channels of healing for others, we are presented with incredible opportunities to help others. Sometimes these experiences may be extremely challenging for our own healing path, but over the years I have learned to just trust Reiki. I knew Reiki had helped the spirit of the deer to pass on. Still, how was I going to sleep tonight with the terrible image of carnage still in my mind whenever I closed my eyes?

After we got home, we took the dog out front for his nightly "pee pee" in the yard before sleep. Usually only one of us accompanies him, but for some reason, this particular night, we were both out on our front walk, waiting for the dog. Suddenly my husband said, "You won't believe this: look!" I looked where he was pointing. It was a truly amazing sight; I had to blink my eyes to make sure I wasn't imagining it. Directly across the street, in the front yard of our neighbor's home, a young male deer stood, quietly looking at us. His 2 straight horns stuck about 4 inches up off the top of his head! After we spent a moment staring at each other, he quietly turned away and walked slowly down the center of the street, until the mist of the evening caused his dark shape to disappear into the distance.

We have lived in this house for over four years, and have never seen a deer in our neighborhood, much less on our street, much less on our neighbor's lawn! This was quite an experience!! I was speechless. My husband said simply, "He came to say thank you."

Yes, this felt right. I have seen many times before, that somehow other animals know and understand that you have helped their cousins with Reiki; amazingly, "word gets out" among animal kind. Also, I knew that this special visit was a gift of healing to my heart. As I lay my head down to sleep that night, I felt hope inside my heart for the wild ones that must somehow live among us. My eyes closed and the only image I saw was that beautiful, peaceful deer, full of grace and life, standing just a few feet away from me. Again, thank you Reiki.

Reiki with an Owl Finch

By Irene Brock

For one of my homework assignments for Kathleen's Animal Reiki Workshop, I decided I would like to work with a wild animal. Since I live in a well-populated area, I headed for the zoo. I arrived shortly after they opened and the weather was windy and cold so I knew there would not be many people around yesterday. Even though I had visions of working with a big animal like an elephant, lion or giraffe, I tried to keep my mind open to working with any animal that would like Reiki. I decided I would walk most of the zoo and then return to the animal hat I felt was most open to me.

I never really considered myself a "bird person" and if I'm short on time I normally walk right past the aviary at the zoo. But in trying to be open to all the animals and also do to the cold wind, the aviary was the first building I headed for. I enjoyed viewing the locals
through the one way glass as they helped themselves to the large bird feeder outside and I considered returning to the bird rescue area that held injured birds that can not be returned to the wild. I continued wandering from room to room and I entered a room that contained about three-dozen small exotic birds with many patterns and colors that were free to fly around the room as they wished. It was not the happy, chirping birds or the brightly colored birds that caught my eye. Sitting, almost hidden by plants, along the walkway was a small, brown and white bird that sat quietly with her (for some reason I felt it was female) feathers all ruffled and breathing heavily and looking quite distressed. I watched for a few minutes as her mate repeatedly approached her and tried to encourage her to feel better. Realizing that I had just gotten to the zoo and had many more animals to visit I left the aviary and continued on.

After an hour or so and visiting many other animals, I could not stop thinking about the little brown and white bird that was so distressed and clearly not doing well. So I returned to the aviary and found her about a foot from where I had left her before. Her mate continued trying to encourage her to feel better. It was such a tender, loving gesture to watch it made my heart hurt for them. I knelt down (I felt I needed to get as close to her level as possible) and began offering Reiki. The room was really soaking up the Reiki energy and she turned to face me. After a short time she hopped on a branch right in front of me and it seemed like we were old friends. She began closing her eyes for longer and longer periods of time. As I sat there, with her at eye level, I saw something that I could not see with her on the ground. There wrapped around her legs was a clear, thin nylon strand that she could not free herself from. At this point I didn't know if I should go for help or continue the Reiki that she was enjoying so much. I also noticed that many of the other birds were moving closer and closer to me and becoming quieter and quieter. It was such a beautiful moment I just had to continue the Reiki for a while longer.

Finally, I couldn't stand knowing what her problem was and not helping her so I went for help. After making another pass through the aviary and not finding a staff person, I left the building and headed for the nearest concession stand. I explained what I had found and asked the worker to call a zookeeper. The teenager went to his manger and asked him to call a zookeeper and the manager nodded in agreement. I returned to my little bird who had now taken shelter in the corner of the room as far away from the increasing foot traffic as she could get. Her mate was still by her side. After waiting another 20 minutes I grew impatient and returned to the non-emotional teenager who again turned to his manager and ask about the zookeeper. The manager said he had forgotten to call and acted like I was bothering him but reluctantly pulled out his radio when he realized I was not just going to go away again like I had the first time. After watching him until he made the call, I then returned to my little bird. Within 5 minutes a zoo keeper was there looking for her and I pointed out the distressed Owl Finch in the corner. The zookeeper agreed she was not doing well.

She went for a net and entered the exhibit through a back door which was right next to my little bird. The bird was startled and flew (which surprised us). The zookeeper called for help and within a couple minutes someone else appeared. With all of us looking, we discovered my little bird and her mate sitting side by side in the shelter of the bushes at our eye level and there shining in the sunlight was the nylon string that bound her legs.

Since well over an hour had passed I left my little bird in the hands of the skilled zookeepers who promised they would take care of her. Of all my lessons I felt this was the most surprising, powerful and rewarding of all.

About the Author: Irene Brock is a Level III Reiki practitioner residing in southeastern Michigan. She also holds certificates as a Spiritual Healer, Lightworker and Feng Shui consultant. Irene is an independent distributor and educator for Nature's Sunshine vitamins and herbs. She may be reached at: healingforce@yahoo.com.

Part 5:
Teaching Animal Reiki

Teaching Reiki For Animals in Your Community:

Reiki I at Animals in Distress Shelter

By John Sawyer
Coopersburg, PA - April 2006

When I first approached the director of Animals in Distress about conducting a Reiki class for the shelter volunteers, she was not familiar with Reiki. I explained what Reiki was and how it had affected my life and the potential it held for working with the animals housed at the shelter. Lois isn't afraid to be out on the leading edge as the concept of a no-kill shelter was considered pretty far out 29 years ago when AID was founded. She said she would run the idea past the volunteers and we would see what interest there was.

As it turned out, the kennel manager had taken a Reiki Level 1 class some years ago and was quite familiar with Reiki. She is also very interested in alternative medicine and holistic living. Another kennel volunteer had had Reiki treatments for arthritis in her hands some time ago and had a good experience with it. A number of the other volunteers expressed interest in learning Reiki, as well. We decided to limit the size of the class to 6-8 people, primarily those who work directly with the animals every day, and had no trouble finding 7 people who were eager to take the class.

I decided before approaching Lois that I would donate the class time and manuals so the class would be free for the shelter volunteers. We adopted one of our dogs from AID and we have been supporting them ever since. They are not a typical shelter in many ways, and we are pleased to help them any way we can.

I donated 8 manuals and 8 multimedia programs to the shelter and these were loaned to the class participants. Those who wished to purchase their own copies were offered that opportunity. The manuals used were Reiki The Healing Touch Level 1 and 2 manuals by William Lee Rand. The multimedia programs were

The Reiki Touch, also by Rand. The latter is billed as a toolkit for the Reiki practitioner and includes a DVD, meditation CDs, a workbook and cards showing the various hand positions. I decided to include it due to the time constraints of the class and because it is an excellent visual demonstration of basic Reiki techniques.

I also purchased 8 copies of the newly published *Animal Reiki* by Elizabeth Fulton and Kathleen Prasad and gave each class participant a copy as a gift from me. This new book is an excellent source of information on treating animals with Reiki and I was very pleased that it became available in time for the class.

We scheduled the class over two evenings, allotting two hours each evening. I felt this was sufficient time to get the class familiar with the basics of Reiki, attune them to Level 1 and have time for some practice. This worked out quite well. As it happened, we finished up within the two hours each night.

I had a bit of a personal issue that I needed to handle prior to the class. As I pulled on a pair of light cotton gloves with little colored circles all over them, I said to the class *"I wish I could sit here and tell you that these are my Sacred Reiki Gloves, however, the truth is that I got into some poison ivy last week and I figured you'd rather be amused than grossed out!"*

Fortunately, they were amused and we enjoyed trading some remarks about how I needed some additional accessories to complete the outfit. The poison ivy also required that I wear long sleeved shirts both nights, contrary to the beautiful weather, but this was a minor inconvenience.

The first night we reviewed the agenda for the class sessions, what Reiki is, what Reiki isn't, the brief history of Reiki, self-treatments, treating others, how treating animals differs from treating humans, and I gave them their Reiki Level 1 attunements.

The students were very interested and asked many good questions. We reached a good breaking point at about 7:45PM and decided to spend the second session primarily working with shelter animals to get a feel for Reiki and how to work with the animals.

The second evening, we began with the Hatsurei Ho meditation and I gave Reiju to each student. After that, I opened things up for questions. The students were very eager to work with the animals to get some hands on experience, so to speak. The hospitality area of the main shelter building is quite large so we were able to spread out to minimize distraction for the animals.

The volunteers brought out dogs and one cat. The volunteer working with the cat decided to take her "patient" into the break room where the cat could be free to roam around without the possibility of a chance encounter with a dog. The rest of us each worked with our respective dogs until the dogs indicated they had had enough Reiki, and then we each got another dog to work with.

My second dog was Max, a Scottie mix who is suffering from lymphosarcoma and heart problems. You'd never know it to watch him as he seems very happy and he's very busy. I have been visiting Max each week for the past several weeks and giving him Reiki to help with his conditions and the side effects of the chemotherapy he has been receiving so he got a bonus session this week.

After I'd finished with Max, I circulated around the hospitality area to see how everyone was doing. The volunteers had questions about whether they were doing the Reiki correctly, and what they should be feeling or not feeling, and what to look for from the animals. All the questions were typical of interested students eager to apply their new knowledge correctly.

One volunteer was concerned that she wasn't feeling much energy flowing, and I assured her that even if she didn't feel much, the dog did and to watch him to gauge the energy rather than relying on her own senses for now. Some of the dogs chilled out and others, like Max, were quite busily engaged with their own agendas, but all the volunteers saw the Reiki affecting their respective animals in noticeable ways. This served to increase their eagerness to put Reiki to work in their interactions with the animals on a daily basis.

We finished up with a group discussion of the healing sessions, and then I handed out certificates, which they proudly displayed for a class picture. I'm looking forward to visiting AID regularly and seeing how the volunteers put their newfound skills to use. I expect there will be additional volunteers interested in learning Reiki once they see the results from this first group, and I'm excited about teaching another class there in the future.

About the Author: Please see p. 60 for details about John.

A Day in the Hay:
Animal Reiki Barn Dance

By Carol Schultz

On a gorgeous and sunny Sunday afternoon recently, there
was a meeting: a meeting of hearts and minds, seeking to come

together and learn from each other, and learn from the animals. I drove up the gravel road to the barn to meet with a small group of members from one of the Animal Reiki class sequences here outside of Chicago. In previous classes over the past two years, we had only worked in person with canine participants during Level 1 of the course, and I had not ventured into taking students to a barn to work directly with horses. However this time, for students in the course interested in learning more about horses, we were being warmly hosted at the barn by Hope, a fellow Reiki Master Teacher, along with several horses at the barn including Dakota, Lady, Frosty, Country Swinger, and Snoopy.

Walking up to the barn, I felt the dirt and rocks of Mother Earth below my feet. My senses and lungs filled with the sweet smell of hay. As I listened to the beautiful chorus of horses serenading our entry, it made adventuring out of the classroom and away from our Reiki notebooks well worth the trip. Not knowing quite what was in store for us aside from my own instructor's outline for the afternoon, the animals had assured me telepathically on the drive there that they knew what to do, and would guide the students well. They said to simply let go and trust, and the students would each receive what they needed for their next step forward with Reiki. It is a wonderful dance of harmony, with horses in the lead.

As Hope introduced the students to the horses, we began to quickly notice their differences in personality and characteristics. Each was clearly a unique individual, inviting us to know them, each with his own story. Over the years of doing animal communication consultations, I have learned that so much of the background of horses becomes unknown as they often change hands from person to person. This is also true of many other species of companion animals as well. It is both interesting and helpful to hear the animals' perspectives on the earlier times of their lives, and what that means to them as part of their journeys. I have found that simply holding a sacred space and allowing the animals to share their thoughts, feelings, and energy can provide profound emotional releases, and assist them in letting go of the past, whatever that might hold for them.

Near the beginning of the gathering, we checked to see which one of the horses was open to working with the group first. Dakota, a very large grey Holsteiner, roughly 18 years old, immediately invited us to work with him. He was described by our host, Hope, as sweet, kind, and gentle, with very giving energy. Unfortunately, he had been abused and beaten prior to becoming a member of Hope's animal family many years earlier.

Due to recent illness, Dakota had been on stall rest, but he encouraged us all to venture in to his stall as a group. As we circled around him and began energetically clearing the space, preparing to work, he encouraged each student to place both of their hands somewhere on his body. He proceeded to explain to the group many aspects of Reiki and working with animals, accompanied by humor and warmth. As students picked up a variation of energetic shifts with his body, Dakota encouraged them to breathe with him through his skin to deepen their spiritual connection with him and this magnificent species. Dakota explained that while the students continued to work with him, he would attune them to horse energy, and help to further open their palm chakras to work with the other horses in the barn, and then ongoing with other animals. It was a very special Reiki attunement for the group from a very special horse, and we felt it was a tremendous gift for him to share. As we completed our connections with him, disconnected energetically, and then exited his stall, he joyfully invited all of us back to work with him further.

After working with Dakota, we were next invited to work with Lady, a 9-year-old chestnut Thoroughbred. It was explained to the group that for a very long time following her adoption at four years old, she could not let anyone ride her. Rather than entering her stall, she was most comfortable having students work with her from the barn aisle. Lady was not sure of everything at first, especially since she was most comfortable having her caretaker, Hope, work with her energetically. She suggested asking for just two students to work with her, and to begin slowly. After a few minutes, she was accepting an increasing amount of Reiki energy, and she loved making the connection with the group. Later on in the afternoon, two participants, Tammy and Tiara, worked with her further, and Lady thoroughly enjoyed her time with them.

In the stall next to Lady was Frosty, a Quarter horse. As the group shifted to work with him, he must have been peeking in at how we began with Lady. Frosty also specifically requested only two students approach, and then begin the Reiki connection from outside the stall. Near the beginning of the session, everyone in the group could sense him hesitating and pulling back, so the Reiki flow was small, and their approach was soft. However after just a few minutes, Frosty began to relax. Claudette and Sandy, the two students from the group working with him, received guidance on where to direct the Reiki around and through his body. They began to feel energetic blockages releasing from his sides and back end, and chakras centers opening up and balancing, while both they and others could provide a description of what they felt releasing from Frosty. By the time we thought he would be finished, based on his hesitancy at the beginning, he continued to ask for more….and more, and more, and more. Eventually, as we needed to complete his session, the students felt him in total acceptance, and he was actually sending energy back to help them as well!

Feedback from Reiki students Tammy and her daughter Tiara, Illinois, August 2006:

We really enjoyed our Animal Reiki work at the barn. We haven't been around horses much so it was a great experience. We were amazed by their intense energy, and how you can feel the horse breathe through every part of their bodies. My daughter and I picked up on one horse's stomach issues and their nervous habits to soothe it. We had to respect the animal's wishes and "turn down" the energy every so often so the horse could take a break and come back when she was ready. We also experienced an incredible gift of one horse giving us energy back. Gratitude is a very important piece of this work. The animals feel it and send it right back. It was a wonderful exchange. We made a lot of great animal connections and we can't wait to do it again! Thanks!

The gift flows both ways between us and the animals. All we need to do is accept their invitation to dance, and share in their world of magic and harmony.

Following the initial guidance and practice with Dakota, Lady, and Frosty, the students were divided into small groups to work independently with several horses, and to document their insights and sessions. Tammy and Tiara continued the work with Lady, Nancy and Sandy started with Country Swinger, a 14 year old chestnut Thoroughbred, and Linda, Mary, and Claudette teamed up with Dylan, an 8-year-old Thoroughbred.

Country Swinger tends to have a tough guy exterior, and *loves* to get attention. He had asked to be included in the small group work, but when they started Reiki with him, he seemed to be much more interested in thinking he was going to receive food. Neither Nancy, nor Sandy felt he was sincerely interested in the Reiki being offered. However, Snoopy, in the stall next to Country Swinger, had made his interest quite clear. Even though he was sometimes considered hard to read or rude, and could be aggressive with groundwork, he was now mister sweet man, putting his nose to the bars and clearly extending an invitation to his party.

Nancy and Sandy concluded their connection with Country Swinger, and accepted Snoopy's request. After they began their work with Snoopy, by the end of a 20-minute session of mostly hands-off Reiki, he was up against the wall in his stall completely relaxed, quite literally "in the zone" and experiencing a deep and relaxing Reiki nap. Hope reported later that Snoopy was lovely and totally calm for the rest of the day.

The third student group of Linda, Mary, and Claudette choose to work together with Dylan, the 8 year old Thoroughbred. Linda, a fellow Reiki Master Teacher and Animal Reiki case mentor, was there to help facilitate. In combination with Mary and Claudette, they made a wonderful Reiki team. Dylan's trainer, Sarah, had asked us for emotional healing help with him since he is aggressive in his stall, displays aggressiveness towards humans, and lunges.

The session with him that afternoon was somewhat surreal. With Dylan safely in his stall, and the three practitioners standing across the aisle, they introduced themselves to Dylan from their hearts and minds, and asked for permission to send Reiki. They sensed hurt, anger, frustrated feelings, and a weak aura field with gray splotches. As Mary and Claudette held the sacred space and facilitated energetic releases with Reiki, Linda proceeded to incorporate positive affirmations, EFT (Emotional Freedom Technique), and long distance Tellington TTouch work.

Here is Mary's description of the session:
I volunteered to work with Dylan, a horse. We were told that he needed a lot of help. As we walked up to Dylan's he said to me "that man." I could see the anger in his eyes, yet he was ready to accept Reiki into his life. When we started the session, he was backed up against the far wall in his box stall, ears pinned back. As we progressed, I could feel his fear, loneliness, and lack of self-worth come to the forefront.

I saw a huge energy bubble well up from his hindquarters, and he eventually showed me his sore neck and shoulders. Then he drank in that beautiful Reiki energy. My heart felt as if it had been pierced by an arrow, and my solar plexus was tightening...I reminded myself to breathe and stay grounded!

I called him a very handsome boy as that powerful, yet safe energy surrounded him within and without, helping him to start releasing what he did not need. He told me that he did not want to go back "there," and I told that magnificent creature he was safe here. When we needed to end our session, he was up in the very front of his stall, relaxing with his eyes half closed, and I thought, "what a phenomenal experience." The stable had grown very quiet, perhaps absorbing the peacefulness of all of the Reiki in the air.

It was an honor to have met Dylan. He touched me in a way that I will never forget, and I am thankful that I chose a path that led me to Reiki. I send a heartfelt thank you to Carol, Linda, and Hope for offering this wonderful practice session, and I look forward to seeing Dylan again and working towards Reiki III.
~ Mary, Illinois, August 2006

Following this orientation day at the barn, some members of the Animal Reiki class volunteered to work with several cases for further practice, and to provide additional assistance to several animals in need. Based on the experience with Dylan at the stables, he was chosen to be one of the continuing student cases. Over the course of the next three weeks, Linda and Claudette were paired to work both in-person and long distance with Dylan, and the results have been both heartwarming and profound.

Approximately a week after the first session at the barn, a small group visited him once again. After energetically cleansing his stall, they helped to release a great deal of blocked energy from his shoulder and solar plexus, and they also incorporated crystal-healing work. When they took a break, Dylan actually encouraged them to restart, and by the end of the session his muzzle could be stroked, and he was at the front of his stall to say goodbye. A wonderful experience for everyone!

Several days later, Linda and Claudette returned to continue Reiki work with him again. After doing Reiki on themselves first and reinforcing spiritual protection, during the session he lunged to the front of the stall three times. One practitioner

Dylan

focused on removing negative energy, while the other sent positive energy. He was clearly accepting the treatment, and both Linda and Claudette sensed that they further gained his trust.

After a few more days, Dylan just wanted to talk. No Reiki, just talk. He discussed how humans don't understand animals. He emphasized the intelligence of animals, along with their feelings and emotions. Dylan also mentioned that the other horses in the barn were curious about the fact that he was talking with humans, and that they were actually listening!

By his sixth Reiki session, Dylan was so anxious to get started, that he interrupted the practitioners' conversation and invited them to come down to his stall. He greeted them politely, and his owner, Julie was now present and participating as well.

Julie could not believe how calm he was, and the Reiki team encouraged her to talk with him. As she did so, they all felt a huge release from his heart. They continued with positive reinforcements, repeating the words of "respect, honor, and love." Showing his apparent agreement of the affirmations being conveyed, Dylan shook his head up and down. After some time, Dylan was getting a bit restless with the amount of Reiki, so the group began gently moving figure eights along his energy, or hara, line to help release any built up energy that wasn't fully flowing. Upon concluding the session, they also sent calming energy to his stall to release any built up emotional energy from his area.

The feedback from Dylan's owner, Julie, has been wonderful, and a tremendous validation for the students. At the end of the most recent session with him at the barn, Julie was moved to tears. Dylan allowed her stroke his muzzle. Julie communicated to the students that in the three years he has been with her as a companion, she has never seen anything like this. She has never has this kind of connection with him, and now Julie feels that she is beginning to sense feelings from him as well.

We thank Reiki for these blessings, and we thank Dakota, Lady, Frosty, Country Swinger, Snoopy, and Dylan for being such wonderful teachers!

Are you ready to learn their dance? The steps are easy, and the animal teachers would love to invite you to their party so you can enjoy yourself and have some fun as well. Listen, and you will hear their voices calling you, like a microphone inside your head. Play some music, relax, enjoy, and slow down, and you'll find them waiting there for you to take some time out and enjoy life!

About the Author: Carol Schultz is an Animal Communicator, Reiki Master Teacher, Shamanic Healing Practitioner, and Interspecies Life Coach. She began working telepathically with animals in 1999 after being drawn to this spiritual role following her decision to make a lifestyle change from her corporate background and career. Carol initially trained with Penelope Smith, and has studied with many other communicators and healing practitioners throughout her journey. Carol is sponsor of the Animal Spirit Healing and Education Network, which hosts Chicagoland area classes including Animal Communication, Animal Reiki, Pet Loss, Tellington TTouch, and Shamanic Healing. Through Animal Spirit Network (animalspiritnetwork.com/index.php), she encourages students being trained in a variety of holistic healing modalities to learn from the animals while assisting with case studies submitted for assistance from area animal shelters and rescue groups. Please visit her website at www.carolschultz.com.

Part 6:
Other Animal
Reiki Topics

Animals as Reiki Healers

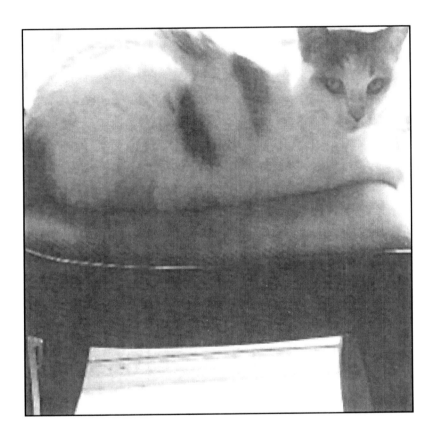

By Nada Rodgers

Animals are intuitive creatures with a natural ability to heal each other and humans in many ways. Their capacity for unconditional love is boundless and their sharing without bias puts me in awe. Companionship for the lonely, protection and healing are just a few examples of their roles in our lives. I believe that this is because animals are natural "Reiki" facilitators.

I was taught that Reiki is defined "universal life force". In my lifetime experience with animals I have learned that animals naturally connect to this energy force and direct it to help each other and humans. Instinctively they can absorb our negative energy (what is causing pain or otherwise) and dispose of it from their bodies. Humans have not always been clear of their intention with animals but animals are always clear with their intention to send energy for only the good of the recipient. I would like to share a few stories of animals helping people with Reiki.

I have been blessed to have experienced healing animals with Reiki and equally blessed with experiencing healing from them. Maggie, my natural healing cat, has helped me to heal others and myself a few times. One day I was laying on the couch working on healing a painful knee that was a problem for over a month, Maggie came up and lay across my knee with her belly flush over the painful area. Her weight was as light as a feather. She stayed there purring for about 10 minutes and then jumped down. My pain was gone and has never come back. Another time I had a client who was about to go for surgery to remove a pancreatic tumor that had a 99% chance of being malignant. During the treatment Maggie once again hopped up and lay across my client's abdomen. When the treatment was done the lady got up and said, "I know I will be fine now." She went for surgery and all was benign.

I have also witnessed animals healing on a more general level. My friend Joan had given her dog up to a friend, as she no longer was physically able to handle her needs. Joan had become somewhat disabled, able to ambulate short distances only and requiring some help for other things. I visited her one day and found her place emotionally dark and cold and Joan herself very depressed. Joan had called and wanted to adopt a cat. I drove her to a rescue centre where Joan immediately was drawn to a year old female calico, who was healing from a wound she had received before she was rescued. Joan did not hesitate; she adopted Mitsy. The next day I visited Joan to see how things were going. What a change! Her house experienced a positive transformation. There was light and happiness; Joan looked like she had been reborn. I believe Mitsy filled the house with Reiki energy when she moved in and brought it back to life. Both are doing well together to this day.

Being attuned to Reiki was the best gift I received in my life. I always feel even more blessed as I learn more from the love and compassion of animals and their ability to send Reiki energy without bias. My house is "Reiki Friendly." Anyone who visits feels better when they leave. My cats make sure of it.

About the Author: Nada Rodgers started practicing Reiki on people and animals over 3 years ago. She currently lives in Ontario, Canada.

Complementary Skills For Your Reiki Practice

By Kat Berard

In my late twenties I became interested in metaphysical studies. Little did I know where this would lead me, and how it would change my life. After taking a number of metaphysical classes, I was drawn to take Reiki and became a Reiki Master. I was amazed at how beneficial this energy healing mode could be and had some very interesting experiences with this involving both animals and people.

Since animals have always been a central theme in my life, over time I was drawn to work more closely with animals in various ways. One of those ways was through animal communication. I knew I had the ability to telepathically communicate with them but had no idea how to consciously operate this. Usually I just "received" a piece of information or a sense of knowing something about them, not really knowing how this occurred. This had been the case since I was a young child, and it was fairly easy for me to tune into psychic or telepathic information about people as well.

It was a big switch for me to move into the world of animal communication because I worked in the legal field at the time. I think that's about as far away as you can get from "the weird and woo-woo" (I use that term with great affection!). I proceeded, knowing I was being drawn along this path for a specific reason. There came a point where I knew this would be the perfect way for me to be in service to animals and their people. The legal field served me well, and I greatly enjoyed that work, but when burnout hit, I knew I could no longer ignore what gave me great satisfaction - serving others from a place of love and respect to assist them on their paths.

Today I am an Animal Communicator and teacher with a worldwide practice, a medical intuitive, and vibrational essences practitioner among other things. I also do intuitive guidance sessions for people, and educate people about holistic animal care.

If someone had told me in high school that one day I would be talking with animals and receiving higher guidance for the benefit of animals and people, I'm sure I would have looked at them cross-eyed. However, it's absolutely perfect for me, and it gives me great joy to be in service to others.

The key point I focus my life around now is, does my work juice me up, make my heart sing, give me deep satisfaction, keep me interested, encourage me to continue growing? I'm always a student, and find that the deeper I delve into holistic, alternative and complementary modes, the more satisfied I become and the more fully I appreciate the path I'm on.

Animal communication is not something for the "gifted few". Telepathic communication is an innate ability we are born with. What typically happens, though, is by about age five, adults shut that down in us by telling us we didn't hear the dog say that, we don't really have an imaginary playmate, we didn't really pick up on the emotions and undercurrents in our parents' relationships, it's not okay to say those things in front of others (public acceptance is more important than the truth) . . . on and on.

For those of us who have gone against the mainstream and opened to alternative or unconventional methods - Reiki, Emotional Freedom Technique, vibrational essences, TTouch, connection with our spirit guides, angels and Higher Self, talking with the animals, seeing spirits, or whatever else comes our way - it can be a daunting adventure to swim against the current of public disbelief or denigration. But definitely worth the journey!

Animal communication can enhance your Reiki practice in a number of ways. Opening to subtle energies and messages from the animals, "seeing" their auras, asking specific questions of the animals to ascertain whether the issue(s) they're dealing with are mental, emotional, physical or spiritual in nature, asking how they can most benefit from Reiki energy (which level do they need healing at?), doing body scans (medical intuitive work), asking the animal if they have a message for their person regarding the issue they're dealing with (I find that many times the animals are mirroring something for their humans) . . . all of these can provide you with more information that may be beneficial in offering Reiki to the animal.

Of course, the animal decides how much healing energy to accept and what it does with that. But knowing the above information may help further guide you in, for instance, how you offer the energy, where you direct it on the body or to the etheric layers (loss of parts of the soul, trauma, illness and other situations can leave gaps, holes or tears in the layers, which may need repair), the intensity of energy that you run, and whether finishing up the session with color therapy is appropriate.

Color therapy is another complementary practice. When I am doing healing energy work on an animal (so far, I've always done this long distance), I scan their aura to feel what color(s) would be most beneficial to them at various points throughout the session and again at the end. I do a clearing first, and the energy drawn off may be sticky like spider webs, gooey, fragmented, black and speckly and angry feeling, heavy and dark or gray, frenetic, . . . it varies. I also look at organ systems, skeletal structure, the part of the body that is diseased etc., and draw off energy specifically surrounding those areas, which may feel different than what is in the aura overall. I then offer Reiki and other healing energies for the animal.

When that is complete, I transmit color energy or vibration to the animal. Oftentimes I will wrap them in a beneficially colored energy cocoon and tell them it's there as long as they want it, and they can draw on that energy at any time. I convey this to the client so they can also visualize their animal in this energy cocoon. Finally, I will make suggestions to the client as to what colors to place near where the animal likes to lay. Although animals don't see the full spectrum of colors through their physical eyes, at the higher consciousness level all things are known, and the Third Eye understands the color energy, so they do benefit from color therapy. A great book for this is *Healing with the Rainbow Rays: The Art of Color Energy Therapy* by Alijandra.

One other complementary therapy I'd like to share with you is vibrational essences. I specifically work with the Bach flower essences and Wild Earth Animal Essences but there are many lines available. These essences work on all four levels (mental, emotional, physical and spiritual). Dr. Bach believed that all physical illness is as a result of dis-ease in any of the other three states. Bach essences gently rebalance those states and can ease physical discomfort. Will it cure, for instance, cancer or arthritis? I can't say definitively, because I have not had an animal client "recover" from such health issues. But, it will help them achieve a state of greater harmony and balance, which can benefit the physical body in some way.

Flower essences are not herbs or drugs; they do not work physiologically in the body like those two do. Rather, they rebalance the energy of a mental, spiritual or emotional imbalance or state of dis-ease. Offering vibrational essence suggestions (or making up treatment bottles for the animal) may help the animal benefit even more greatly from your work. Two books I recommend are Bach Flower Essences for Animals (same title), one by Stefan Ball and Judy Howard, and the other by Helen Graham and Gregory Vlamis.

Blessings to you on your Journey! And bless you for being a Light worker. Namaste, Kat

About the Author: Kat Berard is a world-renowned Animal Communicator and teacher, Reiki Master and energy healer, vibrational essences practitioner, medical intuitive, and host of the weekly Internet radio show, Animal Corner, on www.katberard.com. Please visit her website at www.katberard.com for a list of workshops and classes, to sign up for her free monthly email newsletter, and to find out more about animal communication, what the animals teach us, vibrational essences, essential oils, spirituality, holistic care and much more. You can contact her at kat@katberard.com.

The Animal Reiki Practitioner Code of Ethics:
Supporting the Commitment of Today's Professional Animal Reiki Practitioner

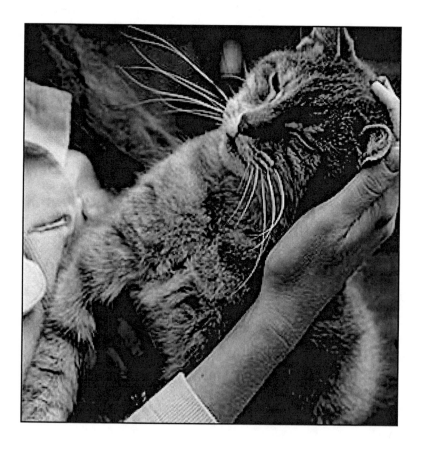

Photo Courtesy of Kendra Luck

By Kathleen Prasad
(Originally published in *Reiki News Magazine*, Fall 2007)

Just a few years ago, it was nearly unheard of to find a Reiki practitioner whose practice was dedicated solely to animal clients. Today, there are hundreds of animal Reiki practitioners starting their businesses all over the world. In teaching so many of these enthusiastic and dedicated practitioners, I found myself motivated to bring together the Animal Reiki Community. Many of us have felt isolated, not only from the animal health field (as Reiki is just on the cusp of becoming well-known in holistic veterinary circles), but also from other Reiki practitioners, who often may ask us, "Working with animals is the same as working with people, isn't it?" Working with animals involves many of the same principles as working with people, but there are some additional factors that deserve mention, including our approach to the animals, our relationship with human companions, and art and nuance unique to the inter species Reiki dialog.

A need began to present itself: a need to define and validate the uniqueness of the work that we do. A need to find a common ground from where to start as professional practitioners, and a language to express what it is that we do from our hearts for the animals--and something to help others know where we are coming from. And so, the Animal Reiki Practitioner Code of Ethics was born.

Before presenting the Code itself, I'd like to share a few words about our commitment as Animal Reiki Practitioners--a commitment that begins with our own healing journey and moves outward to the animals, the animals' families, the animal health profession and the animal community itself. It is this inner commitment that motivates us in our mission not only to bring the wonderful healing of Reiki to the animals in our lives but also, in doing so, to uphold the highest standards and protocols for our new and developing profession.

1: Commitment to Pursue a Healing Path for Ourselves and for the Animals

Animal Reiki Practitioners are committed to personal growth and healing through Reiki. We know that the more committed we are to our own personal practice of Reiki, the more effective we will be as healing channels for the animals. Thus, it is important to incorporate Reiki into our daily lives--to really "make it ours" in an authentic and unique way. The experience of Reiki in our own lives is in essence the experience of the healing that happens in the space of "Oneness".

It is in this space when we realize that we are not separate from the animals, that we can commune and connect with them at the deepest levels, and that we can view the world and its animals with compassion, reverence and gratitude. It is in this space that we find our heart's motivation to be truly committed to animal healing. As we work on our own issues, setting a daily intention for healing, we become clearer and stronger channels for Reiki healing. The animals will sense our pure intention to help them, as well as the energy we offer; it is amazing to see the animals come and ask for a treatment! It is a profound lesson in the intuitive depth of the animals, their energetic wisdom and the connection of all things at their very essence.

2: Commitment to Support the Animal's Family

When we work with animals, we also work hand in hand with their animal companions. In addition, when animals are sick, injured, or otherwise in need of healing, the whole family is affected (both animal and human members). Invite family members (human and animal) to sit in the room with you during the animal's treatment to absorb some Reiki as well. Sometimes human companions may even decide to set up a separate appointment for their own treatments.

There's another reason it's important to see yourself as supporting the whole family, not just the animal client: you are compassionately validating the significance and difficulty of caring for an injured, ill or dying animal, and the importance of the role the animal plays in the family. This is a validation often not echoed in our society.

For example, many human companions of my clients have shared with me that when they went to work after their beloved animal companion had died, if they showed sadness or grief for more than a day or two, people would say things like, "It's only a dog (or cat, etc.). Get over it." Others have shared with me that when they decided to care for their animals despite chronic illness or disease, people would say, "That's a lot of work and expensive too. Why don't you just put him down?" In bringing Reiki to the family, healing, peace and comfort will come to all aspects of the situation, including these.

If you are working with an animal who is very ill or approaching his or her transition, you can find yourself in a very emotional and stressful environment in the animal's home. Everyone in the family will be dealing with the situation differently, and it's important as the healing practitioner that you remain open and accepting of the feelings and needs of each family member. Staying centered and peaceful is important, as you can hold that vibration for everyone, creating a "healing space" in which everyone can feel comfortable to open themselves to the healing that Reiki offers.

Animal Reiki practitioners often receive intuitive information from the animal during treatment. This information may be helpful to the human companions in their understanding of what the animal is going through.

In this case, it is good to share the information with them. It can provide comfort and clarity to the humans, which in turn brings stress relief to their animals. It's also important to remember not to overstep your bounds as the Reiki practitioner: allow the human companions to find their own way, with the advice of a trusted veterinarian, in choosing the journey of the animal. For example, stay open, flexible and without judgment, even in the midst of difficult and emotional decisions, such as the decision to euthanize. Bringing Reiki to the situation will help things unfold in the best way for the animal.

3: Commitment to Support Other Animal Health Professionals and Needy Animals in the Community:

As allies to the veterinary profession, who are the leaders in our community when it comes to the health and well-being of our animals, we must work to create partnerships and cooperative relationships with both veterinarians and other practitioners in the animal health field. This can often be difficult since Reiki is still relatively unknown in the traditional veterinary profession and among many other animal health practitioners. It is important to see ourselves as working in tandem with not only vets, but also other supportive professionals such as animal chiropractors, animal acupuncture and acupressure practitioners, massage therapists, trainers,

Photo Courtesy of Kendra Luck

animal communicators, groomers, pet sitters and dog walkers. All of these people work toward the same goals: happiness, wellness and a good quality of life for our animal companions. Each animal's path to balance and wholeness may require a combination of many healing modalities, to which Reiki can be an integral and supportive component. Building professional alliances, sharing knowledge and creating friendships with other practitioners brings new knowledge, depth and insight from the wisdom of a multitude of healing disciplines to our own work. We can do so much more together than apart.

To further support the community, Animal Reiki Practitioners should reach out to the animals who need it most: those in shelters, sanctuaries and rescue centers. Many of us already donate our time and/or money to these organizations, and so in bringing also the gift of Reiki, we are simply stepping up to a new level of commitment to the needy animals of our community. In donating our time and knowledge for Reiki treatments for the animals and/or classes for the staff and volunteers of these facilities, we receive blessings and gifts from the animals we are helping that outweigh our efforts many times over. Many of Reiki's deepest lessons in animal healing are to be found within the walls of your neighborhood animal shelter, or tucked away behind the fence of your nearby animal sanctuary. In addition, in becoming a valued volunteer to these organizations, we build community friendships that will last a lifetime.

4: Commitment to Educate Others about Animal Reiki:

We are by nature pioneers in this work in the holistic animal health field, and so must learn to educate other animal health professionals and veterinarians about what we do (even if we are not at first comfortable with being "educators"), so that they can understand the value of integrating Reiki into the animal's healing program. This education extends to the human companions of the animals with whom we work: we must learn to create a language about what we do so that humans feel comfortable in letting us treat their "fur kids." This includes explaining what they should expect a treatment to look like and common behavioral reactions to the energy. It also involves letting them know that the animal, not the Reiki Practitioner, is in charge of exactly how (and indeed whether) the treatment unfolds.

Luckily, in addition to the words of our own explanations to people about Reiki with animals, the experience of the treatment speaks even more powerfully than anything we ourselves can say. The animals, so wise and well-versed in the language of energy already (as is their nature), show us clearly in their physical, mental, emotional and spiritual responses not only that they feel the energy of Reiki, but also that they benefit greatly from it. Yes, the animals are often the best Reiki teachers: a lesson learned best when accessed from a place of humility and respect, where the animals are active partners in the process.

We are also pioneers in the Reiki world, as most practitioners have trained and work solely or primarily with humans. Our human-client counterparts are often very interested in the differences in approach and method when working with animals. We can learn from their human treatment experiences. In addition, sharing lessons the animals have taught us can benefit every Reiki practitioner; we can gain insights into Reiki treatments, the profound nature of the healing process, the universal language of energy, as well as life lessons in courage, joy, hope, forgiveness and gratitude, just to name a few.

Animal Reiki Practitioner Code of Ethics

Developed by Kathleen Prasad, Founder of Animal Reiki Source

Guiding Principles:

- I believe the animals are equal partners in the healing process. I honor the animals as being not only my clients, but also my teachers in the journey of healing.

- I understand that all animals have physical, mental, emotional and spiritual aspects, to which Reiki can bring profound healing responses.

- I believe that bringing Reiki to the human/animal relationship is transformational to the human view of the animal kingdom.

- I dedicate myself to the virtues of humility, integrity, compassion and gratitude in my Reiki practice.

In working on myself, I follow these practices:

- I incorporate the Five Reiki Precepts into my daily life and Reiki practice. I commit myself to a daily practice of self-healing and spiritual development so that I can be a clear and strong channel for healing energy.

- I nurture a belief in the sacred nature of all beings, and in the value and depth of animalkind as our partners on this planet.

- I listen to the wisdom of my heart, remembering that we are all One.

In working in the community, I hold the following goals:

- I model the values of partnership, compassion, humility, gentleness and gratitude in my life and with the animals, teaching by example. I work to create professional alliances and cooperative relationships with other Reiki practitioners/teachers, animal health-care providers and animal welfare organizations in my community.

- I strive to educate my community in its understanding of the benefits of Reiki for animals.

- I continually educate myself to maintain and enhance my professional competence so that I uphold the integrity of the profession.

- I consider myself an ally to the veterinary and animal health community. I work to support their efforts in achieving animal wellness and balance. I honor other disciplines and their practitioners.

In working with the human companions of the animals, I will:

- Share information before the treatment about my healing philosophy, the Reiki healing system and what to expect in a typical treatment, as well as possible outcomes, including the possibility of healing reactions.

- Provide a clear policy ahead of time regarding fees, length of treatment and cancellation policy, as well as "postponement" policy, should the animal not want the treatment that day.

- Never diagnose. I will always refer clients to a licensed veterinarian when appropriate.

- Honor the privacy of the animals and their human companions.

- Share intuition received during Reiki treatments, with compassion and humility, for the purpose of supporting their understanding of the healing process.

- Respect the human companion's right to choose the animal's healing journey, selecting the methods, both holistic and/or conventional that he or she deems most appropriate, with the support and advice of a trusted veterinarian.

In working with the animals, I follow these guidelines:

- I work in partnership with the animal.

- I always ask permission of the animal before beginning, and respect his or her decision to accept or refuse any treatment. I listen intuitively and observe the animal's body language in determining the response.

- I allow each animal to choose how to receive his or her treatment; thus each treatment could be a combination of hands-on, short distance and/or distant healing, depending on the animal's preference.

- I let go of my expectations about how the treatment should progress and/or how the animal should behave during the treatment, and simply trust Reiki.

- I accept the results of the treatment without judgment and with gratitude toward Reiki and the animal's openness and participation in the process.

5-Week Audio Course: Download Today!

7 audio downloads and an 8 page journal companion.

Kathleen has created this course for all animal lovers interested in making an inward journey towards energetic and spiritual connections to the wisdom of animalkind. The animals focused on in this course include the wolf, the tiger, the elephant, the bear and the eagle.

http://www.animalreikisource.com/5_power_animal_meditations.html

Other recommended reading:
The Animal Reiki Handbook
by Kathleen Prasad and SARA
Members

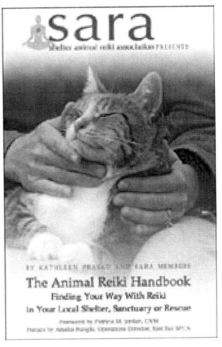

A new nonprofit organization, the
Shelter Animal Reiki Association
(SARA), has published an exclusive
handbook to fill that need. *The
Animal Reiki Handbook: Finding
Your Way With Reiki in Your
Local Shelter, Sanctuary or Rescue*,
published in April 2009, offers
everything Reiki volunteers need to
get started, including an overview
of the organization, mission
and code of ethics of SARA; an

Now Available $14.95

introduction to animal Reiki;
guidelines for working within shelters; and considerations for
treating in a variety of environments.

*"Shelters are often an animal's last hope and a chance at a new life,"
says director Kathleen Prasad, who runs the organization with fellow
director Leah D'Ambrosio. "But for some animals, the stress of
being in a kennel is almost unbearable. With Reiki, I've seen
amazing healing responses—imagine watching a loud kennel full of
hyperactive, stressed-out dogs transform into quiet, peaceful naptime
space. The Animal Reiki Handbook is one way to get more people out
there helping the animals who need it most."*

SARA aims to boost adoption rates in shelters nationwide by reducing stress and supporting healing in homeless animals. The mission will be achieved via a standardized roll-out of animal Reiki programs in shelters worldwide and the creation of an unprecedented global information resource for practitioners and facilities that assist animals in need.

You can find information about ordering *The Animal Reiki Handbook*, along with information and resources about shelter Reiki at SARA's website: www.shelteranimalreikiassociation.org.

About the Editor:

Editor/contributing author Kathleen Prasad is co-author of *Animal Reiki: Using Energy to Heal the Animals in Your Life* and *The Animal Reiki Handbook.* This book represents the second volume of stories collected from her self-published e-newsletter. Kathleen is an animal Reiki teacher, president of the Shelter Animal Reiki Association (SARA), and founder of Animal Reiki Source.

Visit Animal Reiki Source for:

Animal Reiki information
Animal Reiki training programs
Worldwide Animal Reiki Practitioner Directory
A free e-newsletter on Reiki for Animals
A free monthly teleconference, "Animal Reiki Talk"
And much more!

www.animalreikisource.com

"The Leader in Animal Reiki Education"

LaVergne, TN USA
05 September 2010
195900LV00003B/179/P